"Talbot's experience of suffering gives h gles to understand the hard ways of Go(him to voice the most disturbing que .... without minimizing their difficulty or giving in to despair. Talbot uses stories from Scripture to offer the clear practical and theological guidance that suffering believers need to move forward in hope. This beautiful book will comfort readers with the assurance that we are never alone in our suffering but sustained by our ever-loving Savior."

Philip Graham Ryken, President, Wheaton College

"Books offering palliatives to the problem of pain are ten a penny. But this splendid study is different. It is a careful, spiritual, sensitive treatment that does not shirk the emotional and imaginative dimensions of our lives. More importantly, it has to do with human expectations: Jesus said to his disciples, 'In the world you will have tribulation. But take heart; I have overcome the world' (John 16:33). Talbot sets a high standard of fidelity to Scripture as he considers three Old Testament figures— Naomi, Job, and Jeremiah—and the New Testament passages that follow in that vein. So here Talbot is paying particular attention to suffering and the Christian life. This is not a purely theoretical approach to the issues, though it is very thoughtfully written. The discerning reader will have his appetite whetted for the other studies to follow. Unreservedly recommended."

Paul Helm, Former Professor of the History and Philosophy of Religion, King's College London

"If you are a Christian experiencing suffering—or weighed down by the suffering of someone you love—then this book is for you. Talbot—a philosopher-theologian who is also a wheelchair-bound, chronic sufferer—knows what he is talking about. He offers profound, biblical reflections that do not dodge the hard questions or try to minimize the sometimes overpowering reality of pain and loss. *When the Stars Disappear* is a gift to every Christian who is hoping for a reason to hope."

Timothy Larsen, McManis Professor of Christian Thought, Wheaton College

"Through decades of quadriplegia and chronic pain, the Bible has been my source of great comfort and encouragement. And I don't mean only the Psalms or verses about affliction. For me, it's been the stories of godly men and women in the Bible who radiate courage and perseverance despite unthinkable suffering. I have learned how to trust God from their examples, even when painful challenges try to drag me down. It's why I love this new book, *When the Stars Disappear.* Mark Talbot gives the reader a remarkable study of suffering saints and how their mistakes and victories teach us lessons of endurance. I highly recommend this stellar discussion of true Bible stories that will inspire and refresh your heart!"

Joni Eareckson Tada, Founder, Joni and Friends International Disability Center

"*When the Stars Disappear* leads us through a deep, sobering, and powerful encounter with the depths of suffering experienced by three pivotal Old Testament figures. To those who suffer, it offers new hope, comfort, and insight into how to understand and endure such trials with biblically rooted and wise instruction regarding the indwelling grace of God and the ultimate outcome of our journeys. Talbot's unique combination of wisdom, pastoral discernment, biblical fluency, and philosophical and theological mastery combines with his long personal experience of suffering to inform this unique work."

Stanton L. Jones, Provost Emeritus and Professor Emeritus of Psychology, Wheaton College

"I can think of no better way to ask hard questions about the suffering of believers than by delving into the words and stories of Scripture. In this first of four volumes, Talbot dives in deep. He sets the reality of personal, painful experience in the sure context of God's revelation, which not only fully acknowledges Christians' suffering but also lights up hope in God, ultimately through his Son."

Kathleen Nielson, author; speaker; Senior Adviser, The Gospel Coalition

"Writing from the depths of his own experience, thorough understanding of philosophical issues surrounding the theme of theodicy, and careful reading of Scripture, Mark Talbot offers a superb study for people walking through the valley of deepest darkness and for those who function as the Lord's wings to those in distress (Ruth 2:12). With keen insight, an engaging literary style, and a deep commitment to the authority of the Scriptures, Talbot presents a powerful, practical, and pastoral treatment of a subject that we all encounter at some point in life."

Daniel I. Block, Gunther H. Knoedler Professor Emeritus of Old Testament, Wheaton College

"In the face of radical suffering, words often cannot do justice to the gravity of the situation, but sometimes they help us climb through our grief and hold onto the God who has not yet made manifest why such profound suffering surrounds us and happens to us. In this profound and poignant volume, Talbot takes us on a terrifying journey into the depths of suffering to make sure we are brutally honest with it, and to help us understand that our very souls are at stake in clinging to the graciousness of God. This book is not for the faint of heart, but it is for everyone whose lives have been scorched by suffering and do not want to give up."

Richard Lints, Senior Distinguished Professor of Theology, Provost Emeritus, Gordon-Conwell Theological Seminary

"Talbot's unique blend of careful scholarship and distinctively Christian faith and hope are evidenced throughout *When the Stars Disappear*, which serves as a reliable guide and companion to those who have faced calamity. Through Talbot's faithful biblical exegesis and practical theological application, this book is a gift to the church."

Mark A. Yarhouse, Dr. Arthur P. Rech and Mrs. Jean May Rech Endowed Chair in Psychology, Wheaton College

"Anyone who has suffered, regardless of how much, should read this book. It ministered to me. We are reminded to be honest with God in prayer about how we feel about our suffering by, for example, asking God questions like the suffering psalmists do. But then Talbot places our suffering within Scripture's overall storyline of creation, fall, redemption, and new creation, reminding us always to try to understand how God is using our suffering to fulfill that storyline. He explains how our suffering helps us better understand our relationship to Christ and his suffering. By continually going to Scripture, he shows us how saints such as Naomi, Job, and Jeremiah worked through their suffering and came to ultimate trust and hope in God about it."

G. K. Beale, J. Gresham Machen Professor of New Testament, Westminster Theological Seminary

"Many and varied are the books that wrestle with suffering and evil, but in his projected four volumes on the subject Talbot has found some fresh approaches. In this first volume he avoids philosophical and abstract questions, but focuses close attention on a handful of people in the Bible who went through suffering. Their suffering was highly diverse: Naomi, Job, Jeremiah, and some of the psalmists. By leading us through their darkest hours, Talbot lends a personal realism to their sorrow while showing that God often provides life-transforming grace to his suffering people in the midst of their pain, rather than simply taking it all away as fast as possible."

D. A. Carson, Theologian-at-Large, The Gospel Coalition

Suffering and the Christian Life, volume 1

WHEN THE STARS DISAPPEAR

*Help and Hope
from Stories of
Suffering in Scripture*

Suffering and the Christian Life
VOLUME I

Mark R. Talbot

WHEATON, ILLINOIS

Library of Congress Cataloging-in-Publication Data

Names: Talbot, Mark R., author.
Title: When the stars disappear: help and hope from stories of suffering in scripture / Mark R. Talbot.
Description: Wheaton, Illinois: Crossway, 2020. | Series: Suffering and the Christian life; volume 1 | Includes bibliographical references and index.
Identifiers: LCCN 2020024155 (print) | LCCN 2020024156 (ebook) | ISBN 9781433533501 (trade paperback) | ISBN 9781433533518 epdf) | ISBN 9781433533525 (mobipocket) | ISBN 9781433533532 (epub)
Subjects: LCSH: Suffering in the Bible. | Suffering—Religious aspects—Christianity.
Classification: LCC BS680.S854 T35 2020 (print) | LCC BS680.S854 (ebook) | DDC 248.8/6—dc23
LC record available at https://lccn.loc.gov/2020024155
LC ebook record available at https://lccn.loc.gov/2020024156

For
Tory Houriet, Paul Winters, and Buck McCabe

and for

Cindy
To grow old with the beloved of the days of one's youth—
it is this alone that brings truly increasing pleasure in
ever new ways and ever new circumstances.
—Hans Walter Wolff, *Anthropology of the Old Testament*

CONTENTS

TO MY READERS

This book began with my reflection on the horrific tragedy that opens its first chapter. It is the first of four books, each offering a part of the Bible's answer to the questions, Why is there any suffering? Why do Christians suffer? Why am I suffering? and Why is there so much suffering?

Any Christian may suffer, from small children who have just begun putting their faith in Christ to the elderly who may have spent a lifetime following our Lord, from those who have not yet entered elementary school to PhDs.

And any Christian can be puzzled by suffering. So it is important for some of us to address those puzzles by writing books that can be understood by nearly all Christians.

This is what I am trying to do. I want this set of books to be readable by anyone who is willing to think carefully about why Christians suffer. Consequently, I've worked hard to write clear and simple prose, avoiding as much as I can any wording that may discourage someone from continuing to read. Yet at the same time, I haven't tried to diminish the problems that our suffering raises. Trying to say important things simply is not an easy task. The Reader's Guide at the end of the book can help you approach this and the three companion books in worthwhile ways.

This book tries to help you see that your suffering, no matter how awful it may be, is no worse than the suffering that some of God's people have already faced. Their stories, as they are found in Scripture, show us that we are not alone in our suffering. They show that even the most severe suffering can be survived and that we, like these people before us, can emerge from it with our faith and hope in God intact.

I

WHEN THE STARS DISAPPEAR

Man who is born of a woman is few of days and full of trouble.

Job 14:1

Here on earth you will have many trials and sorrows.

John 16:33 (NLT)

The telephone rang about nine on a Sunday morning while we were getting ready for church. I heard the answering machine pick up. As we headed for the garage, I hit the "Play" button. A familiar voice said, "Dr. Talbot, this is Graham. Are you there?"[a] After a couple of seconds of waiting, I heard him say, "Hmm," and then hang up.

It was September. Graham had graduated from Wheaton College in May and then headed overseas for some graduate study in philosophy. He became a philosophy major after taking one of my introductory courses in the fall of his freshman year. We had talked a lot that year. I was encouraged by the depth of his Christian commitment, cheered by his quick humor, and pleased with his sharp, active mind.

---

a. I have changed my student's name and some details of his story to protect his parents' privacy.

For a couple of years after that class, we lost contact. Then I bumped into him at the start of the last term of his final year. He said he would really like to talk. Over lunch he described the depression that had dogged him for years. He had begged God to lift it. But nothing had changed. And so now he was tired, deeply depressed, and uncertain. How could he believe that Christianity was true if God hadn't answered his desperate prayers?

We arranged to talk regularly. He told me he had been in counseling for several years. I had known other chronically depressed students, so I knew how profound their suffering could be. He was grateful when I offered to talk with his parents, which I started doing right away.

Often when I'm dealing with depressed and potentially suicidal students, I ask them to promise they will try to call me at any time, night or day, if they are desperate. Graham had promised, but that Sunday morning he hadn't sounded distressed. After listening to his voice message, I found myself thinking perhaps he was back in the States temporarily and just wanted to get together for lunch.

Monday afternoon I came home from a meeting to find another message, this one from Graham's father. They had received word that Graham had been killed when he was hit by a train. I called them. They had tried to reach the proper authorities, but they hadn't yet been able to learn anything more. I kept my fears to myself. But when I got home the next day, Graham's dad had left another message: it seemed clear Graham's death was a suicide.

As I pieced it together, it became clear that Graham had kept his promise. He had called me less than an hour before he stepped in front of the train.

CALAMITOUS SUFFERING

Profound suffering involves experiencing something so deep and disruptive that it dominates our consciousness and threatens to overwhelm us, often tempting us to lose hope that our lives can ever be good again. A *calamity* is "an extraordinarily grave event marked by great loss and lasting distress and affliction."[1] Both calamities (such as losing a child to suicide) and chronic conditions (such as the continuous care of a severely disabled child or Graham's seemingly never-ending struggle with depression) can produce profound suffering.

Graham's death has been a calamity. Calamities, like earthquakes, start in cores of tragedy that have waves of suffering radiating out from them. For onlookers, the sufferers' lives may soon seem fairly normal again. But for the sufferers themselves, there may be deep inner fault lines that outline shattered faith. The upheavals involved can be so great that it can seem that life can never be good again.

These fault lines often reveal themselves in a series of insistent, unanswered questions. Graham's parents keep asking these:

How could God allow this to happen to our son? We know God is all-powerful and governs everything, so why didn't he alter this course of events?

As Christians we have always believed God is our heavenly Father who answers believing prayer. Yet we prayed believing God would help Graham overcome his depression, so why didn't God help him?

And why did God afflict our son with this burden in the first place, especially since he, as all-knowing, was always aware it would end in Graham's death?

"Why," they ask, "didn't God arrange things so that at least one of the three people whom Graham tried to call in his last hour would have answered the telephone and perhaps helped him find the strength to live another day?"

This book began in response to this calamity. When we stand alongside suffering believers, we face our own questions. In this case, I have asked myself repeatedly, Could I have helped Graham more? Could I have said anything to him that would have made his life more bearable? Were there ways I could have helped him see that God was with him in his dark times even though God didn't take the darkness away? And how can I now comfort his parents? Are there ways to help them weather their profoundly disorienting grief?

Such a calamity reveals how little most of us have thought about what we should say or do in circumstances like these. Does profound suffering have phases that make different responses appropriate at different times? Does intense grief have an early phase when we shouldn't say much, and the best we can do is pray that God will help his grieving children keep their faith? Is it ever appropriate to tell sufferers what many of us have learned through our own suffering, which is that a day will come when they will again feel some peace in spite of their calamity? Should we encourage them to believe they will someday receive satisfying answers to all of their questions? And what should we say to nonbelievers? Is God in some way being good to them in their suffering?

THIS VALE OF TEARS

I will address these questions as we proceed. But no matter how they are answered, all Christians need to come to grips with the potential breadth and depth of what we may suffer. Scripture does not encourage us to believe our lives will be pain free. It shows God's people have always suffered. We can feel profound, life-depleting sorrow.

In Scripture, proper names are meaningful. And so it is significant that even David, whose very name means "beloved by God,"[2] could cry,

> Be gracious to me, O LORD, for I am in distress;
>   my eye is wasted from grief;
>   my soul and my body also.
> For my life is spent with sorrow,
>   and my years with sighing;
> my strength fails . . . ,
>   and my bones waste away. (Ps. 31:9–10)

As Job observed, suffering is a regular part of human life (see Job 14:1), though it comes in different kinds and degrees. Graham's parents have undergone an almost inconceivable calamity, but not all suffering involves experiencing hurts so deep and disruptive that their presence dominates our lives, and even deep and disruptive suffering may not shake our faith. Yet, as Henri Blocher observes, suffering often presents us with a *problem* in the original sense of that word—that is, it throws an obstacle across our paths, "something that blocks our view, for it resists our . . . efforts to *understand* it."[3] So we shouldn't be alarmed or frightened to find ourselves perplexed when we suffer. Suffering often does perplex us, although (as we shall see in chapter 4) this shouldn't surprise God's people.

Readers of the books of Ruth and Job know that God's Old Testament saints sometimes suffered calamitously, just as readers of the Psalms and Jeremiah know that some suffered chronically. And in spite of some Christian teachers' claims to the contrary, we shouldn't expect it will be different for us as God's New Testament people.[4] For we are part of the creation that has been subjected to futility and that groans for its redemption (see Rom. 8:18–25). Hebrews also tells us that God may use suffering to discipline us for our good (see Heb. 12:3–11).

We are also called to suffer for Christ's name (see, e.g., 2 Tim. 1:8 and 2:3 with Phil. 1:29). "Here on earth," our Lord told his disciples in his farewell discourse to them in John's Gospel, "you will have many trials and sorrows" (John 16:33 NLT). The apostle Paul opened 2 Corinthians by observing that he and Timothy were sharing abundantly in Christ's sufferings (see 1:5). Their suffering had in fact been so terrible that they had "despaired of life itself," feeling they "had received the sentence of death" (1:8–9). No wonder Paul declared, "If in Christ we have hope in this life only, we are of all people most to be pitied" (1 Cor. 15:19).

So we Christians should not be surprised if we suffer just as much or even more than non-Christians, since we may suffer in virtually any of the ways anyone can suffer, and we will also suffer more specifically as Christians.

MY STORY

When I was seventeen, I fell about 50 feet off a Tarzan-like rope swing, breaking my back and becoming partially paralyzed from the waist down. I spent six months in hospitals. Initially, I had no feeling or movement in my legs and no bowel or bladder control. I dropped from 200 to 145 pounds because I was so nauseated that I couldn't eat. Once my back had stabilized a little and I had regained some leg movement, the doctors tried to help me regain even more by having me crawl to breakfast each morning. At the time, I had a calcified stone lodged in my bladder that had formed around the catheter I'd needed during the first few weeks. It had been removed, but the undetected stone remained, causing raging bladder infections that made me incontinent. So when they put me on the floor each morning, I would wet myself and, because it was useless to change, remain soaked all day. When I left the hospital after the stone was finally detected and removed, I was able to control my bladder in most situations and walk awkwardly with a cane.

I am now in my sixties, and the consequences of my fall continue to multiply. I have to worry about things most people never even think about. In the last two decades, I sometimes have sleep-robbing leg spasms. And in the last few years my inability to do much walking has depleted the bone density in my hips to the point where, when I fell a couple of years ago, I broke my left hip and became wheelchair bound. Other complications have hindered my traveling, and some have sometimes put my life at risk.

I have thought about God's place in my suffering for over fifty years. Yet it is not primarily in terms of my paralysis that I have learned the most about human suffering. Those lessons have come in other ways. I know, like Graham, what it means to have prayed desperately for God to change some of the more distressing aspects of my life. I have had seasons of profoundly disorienting perplexity when, night after night, sleep fled from me because I was utterly unable to understand how God in his goodness could have been playing any part in what was happening to me. I have experienced hurts so deep and disruptive that they have dominated my consciousness, making me feel I could lose the Christian faith that has oriented me for almost my whole life. Like one suffering psalmist, I have felt like a little owl alone in the wilderness, feeling that my days were disappearing like smoke and my heart was withering away like parched grass (see Ps. 102:3–11). I am not one who jests at scars while never having felt a wound.

MY AIM

Although this book began in response to a particular calamity, it is written for all Christians who are puzzled or distressed by the griefs, troubles, sicknesses, trials, betrayals, persecutions, and afflictions we and others undergo, whether that suffering is acute and perhaps calamitous, or chronic in some potentially overwhelming way, or even if it is simply significant enough to make us wonder why it should be. I hope it will remove some of the obstacles that suffering tends to throw across the path of Christian faith and hope. I want to help you, my fellow Christians, trust that our suffering is part of God's loving care for us as his people, and that we shall ultimately see each piece of it as an *unsought gift* from him, no matter how difficult or perplexing it may now be. I shall show this from Scripture as corroborated by personal experience. As Augustine said, "I feed you on what I am fed on myself. . . . I set food before you from the pantry which I too live on, from the Lord's storerooms."[5]

THE STORY OF A STORM, A SHIPWRECK, AND A POISONOUS SNAKE

In Acts, Luke records an event in the apostle Paul's life that helps us understand our experiences of profound suffering.

When God called Paul from being the church's persecutor to be a gospel preacher, the Lord showed him how much he would suffer for the sake of his name (see Acts 9:10–16). Part of Paul's suffering came during a storm and shipwreck on the Mediterranean Sea (see Acts 27–28). By this time, he was a prisoner being transported to Rome to appear before Caesar. Luke was with him and details for us the hardships suffered during the storm, including the crew's having to throw the ship's cargo and tackle overboard, and everyone being so worried that they didn't eat for two weeks. Eventually the ship ran aground on a reef and everyone swam for shore after the Roman centurion in charge had persuaded his soldiers not to kill Paul and the other prisoners to prevent their escape. As if all that wasn't bad enough, once on shore Paul was bitten by a poisonous snake.

When the Stars Disappear

For us, the main lesson of this story is that God remains in control of everything even when those involved lose all hope. For at one point in this story, Luke remarks that when "neither sun nor stars appeared for many days and the storm continued raging, we finally gave up all hope of being saved" (27:20 NIV). In ancient times, sailors got their bearings by seeing the sun and the stars. So when the storm blotted out heaven's lights, the condition of crew and passengers was indeed very grave. But then Paul stood up, telling everyone they should take heart because God had assured him in a dream that he would appear before Caesar and that in the meantime he would also keep everyone safe.

What happened to Paul and his companions in this storm when neither the sun nor the stars appeared for many days can serve as a metaphor for what often happens to us when we suffer.[6] As I explain more fully in my second volume, God has made us to be *needy* and *wanty* creatures who are constantly on the hunt for various goods—air, food, water, shelter, safety, health, love, and happiness. Pursuing such goods requires our learning how to lead our lives so we can navigate through life in ways that are likely to secure what we want and need. Taking a particular tack on life in order to pursue our wants and needs requires us to get our bearings, much as the sailors in Acts needed to see the sun and the stars in order to navigate the Mediterranean Sea.

A large part of getting our bearings involves our coming to lead our lives in terms of some stories. Stories help orient us by placing us somewhere on an arc or trajectory that has a beginning, middle, and end.[b] Two different kinds of stories are necessary to give our lives their full meaning: a particular story and a general one. The *particular story* is about what our personal lives mean. Each of us needs to believe a story that orients us to the particular people, places, and things around

---

b. For more on the place of stories in our lives, see chap. 4, especially 63–65.

us, describing where we have come from, where we are, and where we think we can go so that we can project ourselves into hopeful futures where we can get what we want and need.[7] The *general story* answers questions about what human life means. For instance, are we the product of blind, meaningless cosmic forces, or have we been created by God to fulfill some specific purpose? Is human life about nothing but making money or pursuing our own personal happiness? Or is it about serving others and believing and obeying God? Metaphorically, these two kinds of stories are the stars that guide us, helping us navigate life's otherwise uncharted seas.

Suffering tends to challenge these stories and shake our confidence. Even a mild headache can make me doubt a small part of my personal story, which assumes that in a few hours I will be relatively pain free. And profound suffering may threaten to blot out completely the light of the stars that are guiding us by making us doubt the general story we have accepted about what human life means. For instance, Graham's parents have found themselves doubting whether God really is our heavenly Father who answers believing prayer. Losing their bearings so thoroughly means losing hope that they can move forward in any meaningful, satisfactory way.

Yet as Luke's account of Paul's and his shipmates' suffering portrays, even if we lose our bearings we shouldn't conclude that God has lost his. God is *provident* over life's storms—that is, he sees the future and *provides* in advance for the needs of his people (see Ps. 107:23–29; Jonah 1:4; Mark 4:35–41). Just as he spoke the sun and stars into existence to illumine and guide us (see Gen. 1:14–19), so he has given us biblical stories like Paul's to help keep our faith, hope, and love alive.

Paul suffered three other shipwrecks, including one involving a night and a day adrift on the open sea. He was imprisoned and repeatedly flogged and beaten as well as stoned. He had been in danger from rivers and robbers as well as from Jews and Gentiles and false Christians. He knew many cold and sleepless nights and hungry and thirsty days. On top of it all, he was constantly anxious for all of the churches.[8] Yet precisely because of what he had learned about God and his faithfulness through all this suffering (see Rom. 5:3–5 with 2 Cor. 1:3–7), he could confidently declare, "If God is for us, who can be against us?" For how will he "who did not spare his own Son but gave him up for us all, . . . not also with him graciously give us all things?" (Rom. 8:31–32). These convictions enabled Paul to believe God when God assured him he would save him and his shipmates. Though the light of this world's sun and stars had disappeared, Paul kept his bearings by believing what God told him in that dream.

Indeed, even before God had shown Paul the remarkable providence of saving him and his shipmates from this terrible storm, Paul was already urging his New Testament readers to trust in the good news God had called him to preach. This good news is the story of the ultimate triumph we shall know in Christ, the triumph of God's keeping us in Christ's love and thus ultimately delivering us from all bad things. Paul's faith in this story resounds throughout the letter he wrote to the Roman Christians not long before his arrest and his perilous trip over the Mediterranean Sea. It comes out in his attitude toward suffering:

> We *rejoice* in our sufferings, knowing that suffering produces endurance, and endurance produces character, and character produces hope, and hope does not put us to shame. (Rom. 5:3–5)

It comes out in his trust in God's perfect providence:

> We *know* that God causes everything to work together for the good of those who love [him] and [who] are called according to his purpose for them. (Rom. 8:28 NLT)

And it comes out in his unshakable confidence that nothing—absolutely nothing!—can separate Christians from the love of God in Christ: "Can anything ever separate us from Christ's love? Does it mean he no longer loves us if we have trouble or calamity, or are persecuted, or hungry, or destitute, or in danger, or threatened with death?" (Rom. 8:35). No! Assuredly not! For "despite all these things," Paul declared, "overwhelming victory is ours through Christ, who loved us" (8:36–37 NLT).

Of course, sometimes these great declarations don't seem to ring true. Sometimes we can be so overwhelmed by what has befallen us that we cannot understand how God could possibly be working through it for our good. How can *this*, we find ourselves asking, be coming from a loving Savior's hand? Sometimes, as it was for Graham as well as how it is now for his parents, it can seem as if our suffering is so bad, so catastrophic, that we cannot imagine how it can ever be part of any "overwhelming victory" that will one day be ours through Christ. So sometimes our suffering does indeed threaten to destroy our faith in the Christian story we have been using to guide us on our earthly ways. Sometimes the stars of faith and hope disappear.

Perhaps you are puzzled right now by your own suffering or someone else's. Perhaps you are in the midst of some great or long-lasting storm of suffering that threatens to blot out heaven's lights and thus tempts you to lose all hope that you will ever see good again. If this is so, then I hope this book's message may play a part like the one the apostle Paul's message played when he stood and told his despairing companions right in the midst of their storm that God had given him a word guaranteeing he would deliver them. Paul proclaimed a message of hope in the midst of hopelessness. He knew that God never loses his bearings, no matter how bad things may seem, and that God would not promise what he could not do. And God did as he said, for God sovereignly controls all of life's storms. He can—*and ultimately will*—see his people safely through even the worst storms. We have his word that when (whether in this life or in the one to come) those storms finally begin to subside and the sky begins to clear, we will look up and once again see the sun and the moon and the stars, and then realize that our loving heavenly Father has been with us all along our way.

2

SUFFERING SAINTS

God's People May Suffer Terribly

So [Naomi and Ruth] went on until they came to Bethlehem.
And when they came to Bethlehem,
the whole town was stirred because of them.
And the women said, "Is this Naomi?"
She said to them, "Do not call me Naomi; call me Mara,
for the Almighty has dealt very bitterly with me.
I went away full, and the LORD has brought me back empty.
Why call me Naomi, when the LORD has testified against me
and the Almighty has brought calamity upon me?"

Ruth 1:19–21

After this Job opened his mouth and cursed the day of his birth.
And Job said: "Let the day perish on which I was born,
and the night that said, 'A man is conceived.' . . .
Let the stars of its dawn be dark;
let it hope for light, but have none,
nor see the eyelids of the morning,
because it did not shut the doors of my mother's womb,
nor hide trouble from my eyes."

Job 3:1–3, 9–10

O LORD, you have deceived me, and I was deceived;
you are stronger than I, and you have prevailed.
I have become a laughingstock all the day; everyone mocks me. . . .
Cursed be the day on which I was born!
The day when my mother bore me, let it not be blessed!
Cursed be the man who brought the news to my father,
"A son is born to you." . . .
Why did I come out from the womb to see toil and sorrow,
and spend my days in shame?

Jeremiah 20:7, 14–15, 18

One of the worst aspects of suffering is the way it tends to isolate us. When great storms of suffering overtake us, our sense of loneliness can become overwhelming. As the clouds close in, we may lose sight of everything but our suffering, making it loom larger and larger. In profound suffering, it is not unusual to feel as if no one else has ever suffered as much.

Suffering should prompt Christians to turn to Scripture, yet it won't if we feel it isn't likely to have much to say about what we are experiencing.[1] A careful reading of Scripture shows, however, that no matter how profound our suffering may be, some of God's saints having suffered as much. The seas of suffering are not uncharted. This chapter charts how three Old Testament saints fell into the depths of despair. It closes with Jeremiah finding his suffering to be so terrible that he dissolved into God-accusing, life-cursing despair. When you read this chapter's last lines, you may not want to turn the page to start the next chapter. Yet that is exactly what we need: We need to feel Scripture plumbing the life-despairing depths of human suffering.

Initially this may seem discouraging. Misery loves company, but mere company isn't good enough. We need to know more than that others have suffered too. We need to know how to maintain our faith and hope even in the midst of our suffering. And we need assurance that God will carry us through. So turn the page and keep reading! Chapter 3 will offer some breathing lessons for sufferers from the Psalms. And then Chapter 4 will complete the stories of these three Old Testament saints in order to show how God delivered them.

Telling these stories will clarify that suffering has been near the center of a biblical outlook almost from the start. It has never surprised God, and so it shouldn't surprise us.

A STORY FROM RUTH: NAOMI'S DISFIGURING GRIEF

The events recounted in the first chapter of the book of Ruth clearly constitute a personal calamity. Because of a famine in Judah, Elimelech took his wife Naomi and their two sons to sojourn in Moab, where he died and the sons took Moabite wives. Naomi's sons then died before producing children, so she was left a childless widow in a strange land. In ancient times this was perilous. And, in fact, Naomi expressed her hopelessness by trying to stop her daughters-in-law from returning with her to Bethlehem (see 1:8–13).

As was customary with God's Old Testament people, Naomi took her suffering to be divinely ordained, which she expressed in terms of "the hand of the LORD [having] gone out" against her, the LORD having "brought [her] back empty" to Bethlehem, the LORD having "testified against" her, as well as "the Almighty [having] brought calamity" upon her (vv. 13, 21). These phrases—and particularly the last two—suggest she also believed that God was punishing her for some sin.[2] Depending on how we construe the Hebrew, the women of Bethlehem's surprised "Is this Naomi?" upon her arrival back home may suggest that Naomi's calamity had weighed so heavily on her that she was almost unrecognizable (1:19). In any case, given the significance of personal names in the ancient Near East, Naomi's reply, "Do not call me Naomi" (which means *pleasant*); "call me Mara" (which means *bitter*), "for the Almighty has dealt very bitterly with me" (1:20), shows that she felt that bitterness would characterize the rest of her life. For the entire time period covered in the first chapter of Ruth, the woman whose name meant "pleasant" lost all hope her life would ever be pleasant again.

We can't know much about Naomi's mental state as she asked for a name change. Yet in spite of the role she took God to be playing in her suffering, she may not have been doubting his goodness or leaning toward disobedience.[3] If she wasn't, then her life shows that even profound suffering does not inevitably undermine a believer's faith or lead to rebellion.

JOB'S STORY: HIS DEATH WISH

Sometimes suffering shakes a believer more deeply. For instance, Job's suffering prompted him to curse both the night he was conceived and the day he was born (see Job 3:1–3). He asked God why he had ever brought him out of the womb and declared it would have been better if he had never existed (see 10:18–19). We tend to make claims like these when what is happening to us seems so bad that we think there is no hope that our lives can ever be good again.[4] And, indeed, at one point Job declared he would "never see happiness again" (7:7 NIV).

It is important to read these words in context: God himself considered Job "blameless and upright" (1:8; 2:3), despite his imperfections. He had blessed Job with immense wealth and ten children.[a] Yet in one day Job lost his wealth and children (see 1:13–19). Initially, this horrific turn of events threw him into intense yet worshipful mourning: "Naked I came from my mother's womb, and naked shall I return. The LORD gave, and the LORD has taken away; blessed be the name of the LORD" (1:21). But then he fell prey to an excruciatingly painful and disfiguring disease that covered him with "loathsome sores from the sole of his foot to the crown of his head" (2:7). He became so repulsive that his wife advised him to curse God and die (see 2:9).[5] In fact, he was so disfigured that the friends who came to comfort him did not immediately recognize him (see 2:12). And when they finally began speaking to him, they increased his suffering by assuming that it proved God was reproving him for sin.

---

a. As Job himself described it, "The Almighty was . . . with me, . . . my children were all around me, [and] . . . my steps were washed with butter" (29:5–6).

In this horrid situation, Job quickly reached the point where he just wanted to die:

> Why is light given to him who is in misery,
>> and life to the bitter in soul,
> who long for death, but it comes not,
>> and dig for it more than for hidden treasures,
> who rejoice exceedingly
>> and are glad when they find the grave?
> Why is light given to a man whose way is hidden,
>> whom God has hedged in?
> For my sighing comes instead of my bread,
>> and my groanings are poured out like water. . . .
> I am not at ease, nor am I quiet;
>> I have no rest, but trouble comes. (3:20–24, 26)

When his friends began speaking to him, they assumed his suffering proved that God was punishing him. This made him struggle to find words to express his feelings. He declared that if his calamity could be weighed, then it would weigh more than the sand of the sea (see 6:2–3). He said God's arrows were in him, poisoning his spirit, and all of God's terrors were lined up against him (see 6:4). This led him to pray that God would just kill him (see 6:8–9). Each moment of human existence began to look hard and hopeless, especially the sleepless, terror-filled nights:

> Has not man a hard service on earth,
>> and are not his days like the days of a hired hand?
> Like a slave who longs for the shadow,
>> and like a hired hand who looks for his wages,
> so I am allotted months of emptiness,
>> and nights of misery are apportioned to me.
> When I lie down I say, "When shall I arise?"
>> But the night is long,
>> and I am full of tossing till the dawn. . . .
> When I say, "My bed will comfort me,

> my couch will ease my complaint,"
> then you scare me with dreams
> and terrify me with visions. (7:1–4, 13–14)

Consequently, he declared, he would prefer strangling and death (see 7:15). The fact that God would not let him catch his breath filled Job with such bitterness that he loathed his life (see 9:13–21). It seemed that every comfort including the comfort of death had been denied him.

Like Naomi, Job took life's joys and sorrows as God-given and thus believed that God was responsible for his suffering (see 1:21; 2:10). Yet from these truths, it was only a short misstep to conclude that God was not being good to him. He seems to have taken that step somewhere in the first cycle of exchanges with his friends, probably when he began addressing God in the second person:

> Am I the sea, or a sea monster,
>   that you set a guard over me? . . .
> I loathe my life; I would not live forever.
>   Leave me alone, for my days are a breath.
> What is man, that you make so much of him,
>   and that you set your heart on him,
> visit him every morning
>   and test him every moment?
> How long will you not look away from me,
>   nor leave me alone till I swallow my spit?
> If I sin, what do I do to you, you watcher of mankind?
>   Why have you made me your mark?
>   Why have I become a burden to you?
> Why do you not pardon my transgression
>   and take away my iniquity? (7:12, 16–21; cf. 10:1–22)

At the least, it seems, Job felt God was being too strict with him.

EPISODES FROM JEREMIAH'S LIFE STORY: HIS ASSAULT ON GOD

It can get worse. While Job seems to have felt that God was being too strict with him, he never seems to have doubted God's righteousness.

As bitterly as he complained, he seems to have believed that if he could appear before God, he would get a fair shake (see Job 23:1–10).[6] The circumstances surrounding Jeremiah's suffering, however, led him to malign God's character and, at least temporarily, abandon his faith and renounce his calling.

Telling his story takes time, but the lessons we will learn are worth it.

Jeremiah's Life

Jeremiah's suffering was much worse than Naomi's or Job's. Theirs occupied intervals in otherwise pleasant lives. His was virtually the only reality he knew. God had consecrated Jeremiah to be a prophet from before his birth and then, while he was just a teenager, had given him a message that ran against all that his countrymen wanted to hear (see Jer. 1:5–10, 13–19). God also commanded him to stand apart from his people, forbidding him to marry (see 16:1–2)[7] and prohibiting him from mourning with his countrymen or showing them any sympathy (see 16:5). He was not to pray for them (see 7:16; 11:14; 14:11) or to feast, eat, or drink with them (see 16:8). Instead he sat alone, filled by God with indignation at their sins (see 15:17), because his life as well as his words were to foreshadow the sort of desolate barrenness that God was going to visit on his apostate people.

As could be expected, Jeremiah's countrymen reacted with hostility, ridicule, ostracism, threats, plots, and persecution. In his entire book, only four people helped him. Everyone else mocked him and constantly laughed at him (see 20:7). Indeed, he became "a household joke" because he could not stop himself from preaching his message of doom even while God delayed its fulfillment (17:15–16 with 20:8 NLT). As he put it, "I am hated everywhere I go" (15:10 NLT). In addition, the people of his home village, including his brothers (see 12:6), threatened him and secretly plotted to kill him (see 11:18–19, 21; 18:18, 22–23). At one point as the weight of his mission bore down on him, he pled with God, "LORD, don't terrorize me!" (17:17 NLT).

Jeremiah's Curse

These incidents are recounted in Jeremiah's "confessions"—a series of laments he made where he complained to, pleaded with, and sometimes even attempted to incriminate God as he expressed his confusion, anger, bitterness, and anguish over fulfilling his prophetic calling.[8] His distress and anxiety grew until they climaxed in the crisis of faith recorded in Jeremiah 20 when, after he had delivered one of his most graphic predictions of disaster for the kings and people of Judah and Jerusalem, Pashhur the priest attacked him and had him tortured. Afterward, Jeremiah lamented God's having called him to be a messenger of judgment:

> Cursed be the day
> > on which I was born!
> The day when my mother bore me,
> > let it not be blessed!
> Cursed be the man who brought the news to my father,
> "A son is born to you." . . .
> Let that man be like the cities
> > that the Lord overthrew without pity;
> let him hear a cry in the morning
> > and an alarm at noon,
> because he did not kill me in the womb;
> > so my mother would have been my grave,
> > and her womb forever great.
> Why did I come out from the womb
> > to see toil and sorrow,
> > and spend my days in shame? (20:14–18)

These curses are worse than Job's because Jeremiah knew that God had set him apart and appointed him as a prophet from before his birth. Consequently, in cursing his birth he was cursing his prophetic call. Moreover, he cursed his birth by cursing a person—a human being made in God's image—and he cursed this person for not doing what God himself prohibits, that is, murder another human being.[9] In contrast, Job "never sinned by cursing anyone or by asking for revenge" (Job 31:30 NLT).

Jeremiah's Doubts about God

In rejecting his call, Jeremiah, like Job, was denying God's goodness to him. Yet he also seems to have doubted God's goodness more radically.

These doubts seem to stem from how Jeremiah had understood his original call. When the Lord first called him, Jeremiah had replied that he was too young to know what to say. But God had told him his age didn't matter, "for to all to whom I send you, you shall go, and whatever I command you, you shall speak" (Jer. 1:7). God had also commanded Jeremiah not to fear anyone because he would be with him to deliver him (see 1:8). He had said, "Get yourself ready! Stand up and say to them whatever I command you" (1:17 NIV), adding, "And I, behold, I make you this day a fortified city, an iron pillar, and bronze walls, against the whole land, against the kings of Judah, its officials, its priests, and the people of the land. They will fight against you, but they shall not prevail against you, for I am with you . . . to deliver you" (1:18–19). God had even warned Jeremiah, "Do not be terrified by them, or I will terrify you before them" (1:17 NIV).

This warning was probably in Jeremiah's mind as he obeyed God's instructions recorded in chapter 19. God told Jeremiah to buy a clay jar and then take some of the civic and religious leaders of Judah out to the valley of the Son of Hinnom at the entry of the Potsherd Gate.[10] He was then to declare that God was going to bring a disaster on Jerusalem that would make "the ears of everyone who hears of it . . . tingle" (19:3). The valley would become known as the Valley of Slaughter because God's people had forsaken him and profaned the valley with offerings to foreign gods and child sacrifice. The Lord would frustrate all his apostate people's plans,[11] cause them to fall by the sword at the hand of their enemies, and let the birds and beasts feed on their dead. He would make Jerusalem a horror to those passing it, a place remembered for the fact that its inhabitants had succumbed to cannibalism. Jeremiah was then to smash the jar in front of the priests and political leaders, declaring, "Thus says the LORD of hosts: So will I break this people and this city, as one breaks a potter's vessel, so that it can never be mended. . . . Thus will I do to this place . . . and to its inhabitants, making this city like Topheth" (19:10–12).ᵇ

Jeremiah then returned to the temple's court in Jerusalem and proclaimed, "Thus says the LORD of hosts, the God of Israel, behold, I am bringing upon this city and upon all its towns all the disaster I have pronounced against it, because they have stiffened their neck, refusing to hear my words" (19:15).

This horrific prophecy predicted Jerusalem and Judah would suffer the covenant curses pronounced by Moses in Deuteronomy (see esp. Deut. 28:25–26, 36–37, 53–57). It indicted the whole nation and all its leaders. But rather than causing God's people to repent, it prompted them to hate God's true prophet even more, provoking Pashhur to have Jeremiah tortured.¹² When it ended, Jeremiah lashed out at God:

> You deceived me, LORD, and I was deceived;
>   you overpowered me and prevailed. (20:7 NIV)

No other biblical saint attacked God's character so brazenly. The psalmists often complained to God about situations they knew he controlled and which he thus could have alleviated (see, e.g., Pss. 6:2–3; 42:9; 44:23–26; 102:1–11). Yet while they questioned what God was doing (see, e.g., Pss. 13:1–2; 119:84), they never defamed him.¹³

It isn't entirely clear what Jeremiah meant by his words, but at the very least they seem to refer to God's initial promise to deliver him from opposition. It seems that in the shock and pain of Pashhur's mistreatment of him, Jeremiah came to believe that God had broken that promise. It seems he had thought God had promised not to let anyone ever lay a hand on him. As he obeyed his prophetic calling, he became increasingly aware of how much enmity his message produced, and so at least once before, he had regretted his birth and questioned God's dependability (see Jer. 15:10–18). But then God had rebuked him and called him to repentance, reiterating his initial promise and even adding that "I will deliver you out of the hand of the wicked, and redeem you from the grasp of the ruthless" (15:21). Jeremiah had heeded that rebuke and soldiered on, even when it

---

b. Topheth was probably a local overcrowded cemetery.

meant delivering the prophecy recorded in chapter 19. As he did, he must have worried about the reaction it might bring. Yet he obeyed, probably holding God's words from 15:21 in mind. Then Pashhur attacked him, and what Jeremiah thought God had promised vanished like smoke in the wind. A man being tortured certainly does not see himself as a fortified city, an iron pillar, and bronze walls against his opponents. He does not feel he is being delivered from the hands of the ruthless.[14]

Jeremiah's words indict God in a way that Job never did. Job's suffering fostered false beliefs about his future and God's posture toward him, but Jeremiah's ordeal incited him to malign God's character.

Jeremiah's Frustration in Ministry

In the moment's intense pain and psychological shock from having been beaten and then wrung out on the rack, Jeremiah apparently began seeing his whole life story as one long misery resulting from God having unfairly prevailed upon him in his youth. He accused himself of gullibility when he allowed God to entice him into his life of prophecy,[c] which had led to his current intolerable situation:

> Now I am mocked every day;
>> everyone laughs at me.
> When I speak, the words burst out.
>> "Violence and destruction!" I shout.
> So these messages from the LORD
>> have made me a household joke.
> But if I say I'll never mention the LORD
>> or speak in his name,
> his word burns in my heart like a fire.
>> It's like a fire in my bones!
> I am worn out trying to hold it in!
>> I can't do it! (20:7–9 NLT)

Since no one was taking his prophecies seriously, Jeremiah tried to renounce his prophetic office.[15] Yet he found he could not stop speaking.

---

c. As the NLT translates 20:7: "O LORD, you misled me, and I *allowed myself* to be misled."

He was pressing his message in a way that made everyone jeer him, but even then he could not hold his message in.

The next verse spells out the fix Jeremiah found himself in:

> I have heard the many rumors about me.
>> They call me "The Man Who Lives in Terror."[d]
> They threaten, "If you say anything, we will report it."
>> Even my old friends are watching me,
>> waiting for a fatal slip.
> "He will trap himself," they say,
>> "and then we will get our revenge on him." (20:10 NLT)

Jeremiah's isolation prompted all sorts of rumors about him, some of them probably linked to his singleness.[16] His unfulfilled prophecies emboldened people to spit God's words back at him. After Pashhur released him, Jeremiah had said, "Pashhur, the LORD has changed your name. From now on you are to be called 'The Man Who Lives in Terror.' For this is what the LORD says: 'I will send terror upon you and all your friends'" (20:3–4 NLT). Now these very words that the Lord had commanded him to speak were being cast back on him. But the cruelest cut may have involved knowing that even his old friends had lost patience with him. Because Jeremiah's ministry had begun with a blast of negative preaching that predicted disaster for God's apostate people (see, e.g., 2:1–37) but that had remained unfulfilled for over twenty years (see 25:3), they suspected he was a false prophet. They were waiting for him to prophesy something clearly untrue, which could then lead to his execution (see Deut. 18:20–22), and then they would be rid of him.

Jeremiah may have shared their suspicions. He had been prophesying "terror is on every side" for many years (Jer. 6:25), envisioning a divine judgment descending on Judah and Jerusalem so terrible that it would amount to a divine unmaking:

> I looked on the earth, and behold, it was without form and void;
>> and to the heavens, and they had no light.

---

d. In Hebrew Jeremiah's opponents started calling him *Magor*, which the NLT translates as "The Man Who Lives in Terror" and the ESV and NIV translate as "Terror on Every Side."

I looked on the mountains, and behold, they were quaking,
  and all the hills moved to and fro.
I looked, and behold, there was no man,
  and all the birds of the air had fled.
I looked, and behold, the fruitful land was a desert,
  and all its cities were laid in ruins
  before the Lord, before his fierce anger. (4:23–26)

When he preached these words, it seems he thought at least one enemy tribe from the kingdoms of the north was already on its way, as the verb tenses in this passage suggest:

Declare in Judah, and proclaim in Jerusalem, and say,
"Blow the trumpet through the land;
  cry aloud and say,
'Assemble, and let us go
  into the fortified cities!'
Raise a standard toward Zion,
  flee for safety, stay not,
for I bring disaster from the north,
  and great destruction.
A lion *has gone up* from his thicket,
  a destroyer of nations *has set out*;
  he *has gone out* from his place
to make your land a waste;
  your cities will be ruins
  without inhabitant." (4:5–7)

Indeed, the coming destruction appeared so imminent to Jeremiah that it gave him something like a heart attack:

Oh, my anguish, my anguish!
  I writhe in pain.
Oh, the agony of my heart!
  My heart pounds within me,
  I cannot keep silent.

> For I have heard the sound of the trumpet;
> I have heard the battle cry. (4:19 NIV)

Yet the predicted invasion had not materialized, raising the possibility that Jeremiah was indeed a false prophet.[17]

Jeremiah's Complete Disorientation

By the time of the events reported in Jeremiah 20, it was clear that Jeremiah could continue believing in his mission only by radically rethinking how it was going to play out. He had always been uncomfortable proclaiming doom (see, e.g., 15:10 and 17:16 NLT, NIV). Pashhur's attack had made the joys and delights that Jeremiah had reaped from studying God's words, believing his promises, and being God's person (see 15:16) seem inadequate to counterbalance the accompanying pains and sorrows. Indeed, he seems to have at least temporarily believed that the pain and shame made his ministry simply too great to bear. He had once seen God as a fountain of living waters (see 2:13), but now it appeared that God was perhaps no more than a deceitful brook, full in spring but dry as summer came (see 15:18).

Jeremiah's doubts about God and his prophetic mission threw him into a full-blown identity crisis. He found himself doubting the personal story that had given his life its meaning from his youth. His disorientation wasn't prompted merely by the lack of success attending his prophetic work. The intensity of his suffering was tempting him to doubt Israel's story and thus abandon his faith and the beliefs and values that had always oriented him. He was "no longer at one with his office and his tasks" and thus unable to tell himself satisfactory stories about his life and his world.[18] As he stopped trusting God, the stars disappeared, darkening his life and his future.

In that dark moment, Jeremiah seems to have temporarily rallied in believing that God would keep his promise and vindicate him (see 20:11–13).[19] But then he cycled back into life-cursing despair, abandoning all hope that his life and prophetic ministry would end well (see 20:14–18).

So as the events recorded in Jeremiah 20 drew to a close, it appeared to Jeremiah as if he was caught in a double bind: fulfilling his prophetic office seemed to involve unbearable emotional and physical strain, yet attempting to abandon it proved impossible. Neither course seemed feasible and yet both appeared fraught with inevitable suffering. And thus we see the strains of being God's messenger of judgment taking its full toll on Jeremiah, and we see what seems to be the complete collapse of his faith and hope and strength: "Why did I ever come out of the womb to see trouble and sorrow *and to end my days in shame?*" (20:18 NIV).

BREATHING LESSONS

How to Survive Great Suffering

And even if I summoned [God] and he responded,
I'm not sure he would listen to me.
For he attacks me with a storm
and repeatedly wounds me without cause.
He will not let me catch my breath,
but fills me instead with bitter sorrows.

Job 9:16–18 (NLT)

I am worn out waiting for your rescue,
but I have put my hope in your word.
My eyes are straining to see your promises come true.
When will you comfort me?
I am shriveled like a wineskin in the smoke,
but I have not forgotten to obey your decrees.
How long must I wait?

Psalm 119:81–84 (NLT)

If we have found our chief delight in listening to God's word, resting in what we have taken as his promises and trying to do his will, then Jeremiah's predicament may be especially poignant. For we, too, may have suffered a calamity that has drained all of the joy and certainty from Christian living, making everything seem meaningless at best. And then we, too, may be tempted to lash out at God because he seems to have forsaken or betrayed us.

Several years ago when my walking worsened, I began seeing a physical therapist. Often when she asked me to do something difficult and I was straining really hard to do it, she'd say, "Breathe!" Of course, I'm not the only one who has needed to hear that. Women in labor and athletes in training often need to be urged to breathe.

Sufferers sometimes need the same reminder, for thinking God has forsaken or betrayed us involves losing our perspective, which can make it seem as if everything is closing in on us so we can hardly breathe (see, e.g., Ps. 69:1–2). In particular, we can forget to breathe in the words God has breathed out to tell us who he is and why he won't abandon us (see, e.g., Isa. 43:1–3; Eph. 2:1–10), as well as to remind us more generally of what he has—and hasn't—promised.

At one point, Job lost all perspective, accusing God of keeping him from catching his breath (see 9:18). Yet as awful as his situation was, his story finally conveys that what he really needed to hear was, "Breathe! Don't panic! Slow yourself down! Don't take everything to be as it seems. Don't rashly conclude that things can never get better. And, above all, don't conclude that God has forsaken or betrayed you." In other words, Job needed some breathing lessons.

When we suffer, we may too. So here are some lessons, gleaned from Scripture.

LAMENT IN THE PSALMS

Many of us have been encouraged to read the Bible as if its chief purpose is to tell us how to live immediately satisfying lives. This warped view of Christianity holds that life invariably unfolds more smoothly once we accept Christ and start obeying the Bible's directives for godly living.

It portrays those directives as promises that ensure prosperity to those who follow them.

Scripture proclaims that whatever God promises is true because he never lies (see Titus 1:2). But what does God promise? In our eagerness to avoid suffering, we can be like children who think their parents have promised something when they have not. This can lead us to think God has broken a promise when we suffer. But God has never promised that his saints won't suffer. In fact, our Lord warned his disciples that everyone would hate them because of him (see Mark 13:13), telling them that "in this world you will have trouble" (John 16:33 NIV).

The Scriptures are rife with saintly suffering. In addition to Old Testament cases like Naomi's, Job's, and Jeremiah's, the New Testament records much Christian suffering, including Stephen's martyrdom (see Acts 6–7) and Paul's litany of afflictions, trials, woes, and weaknesses in 2 Corinthians (see 1:3–11; 11:23–12:10). Peter also mentioned the many griefs his readers were experiencing, which proved their faith was genuine and thus worthy of receiving "praise and glory and honor" at our Lord's return (see 1 Pet. 1:6–7). Moreover, some passages stress that God's saints can't always make sense of what they see (see Job 21; Eccles. 7:15; 8:14–17; Jer. 12:1–4).

Yet we can read these passages without appreciating them. And so we like Job may feel breathless when we suffer. To expect we won't suffer—or at least won't suffer profoundly—becomes, then, a breathtaking error.

The psalmists can help here, for they often had similar expectations. Then suffering would strike, sometimes taking their breath away. But then they did something remarkable. They filled their spiritual lungs by breathing in the words that God had breathed out for them[a] and then cried to him for grace and mercy by breathing out their sorrows, perplexities, and complaints. "I am severely afflicted; give me life O LORD, according to your word! . . . I rise before dawn and cry for help; I hope in your words" (Ps. 119:107, 147).

---

a. "All Scripture is breathed out by God and profitable for teaching, for reproof, for correction, and for training in righteousness" (2 Tim. 3:16; cf. Rom. 15:4; 1 Pet. 1:20–21).

The psalms expressing such sorrows, perplexities, and complaints are called the *psalms of lament*, and they outnumber every other kind of psalm, totaling over a third of the Psalter. In them the psalmists described to their Lord the feelings that it would have been spiritually harmful for them to try to hide and hold in. Suffering should prompt us to pray, so it shouldn't surprise us to find so much perplexity and distress expressed in a book often called "the prayer book of the Bible."[1] Studying these laments teaches us to breathe in at least two ways.

Breathing Lesson 1: Pray

Profound suffering can stifle our prayers by overwhelming us and by tempting us to think that God mustn't care if he didn't prevent this pain.

The laments show that this is exactly what we shouldn't allow our suffering to do to us, for they are prayers seeking personal contact with God.[2] Of course, prayer can be wordless, as when the Holy Spirit helps us pray by interceding "with groanings too deep for words" (Rom. 8:26; cf. Ps. 77:4). Yet it usually involves words and addresses God as "you."

These psalms teach us to take all our sorrows, perplexities, and complaints straight to God. The psalmists never talked *about* God in their suffering; they always spoke *to* him.[3] No psalm of lament complains about God by referring to him in the third person—in other words, the psalmists never gossiped about God or talked about him behind his back. They always complained directly to their Lord. This made their laments acts of faith, for they were appealing to the special, personal relationship they had with him and then showing him the respect of addressing him as the righteous, faithful person he was and trusting he would act accordingly. We must do the same.

If prayer necessarily addresses God, then it is a bit misleading to call Psalms the Bible's prayer book, for almost a third of the psalms don't address him. They address us, urging us, for instance, to praise him for his mighty deeds and excellent greatness.[4]

Yet this throws the laments into greater contrast, for of the remaining 106 psalms that actually involve prayer, about fifty-nine are individual or community laments, outnumbering all the other prayers.[5] They arose from a sense that something in life was wrong, that something was out of tune with the way the psalmist, as a believer, thought, wished, or felt life should be. This was sickness or old age (see Pss. 88:15 NLT; 71:9, 18), psychological distress,[b] spiritual anguish (see Pss. 39; 51:1–3; 130:1–3), opposition by enemies and evildoers (see Pss. 3:1–2; 6:7; 7:1–2), or some combination of these (see Pss. 71; 102).[6] Noting the range of experiences the psalmists lamented helps us to anticipate something of the range of suffering we, as God's present-day people, may also face.

These prayers possess an urgency the other prayer psalms lack. In all but ten of them, God is invoked directly in the psalm's first few words: "LORD, do not rebuke me in your anger or discipline me in your wrath" (Ps. 6:1 NIV). "O LORD, I call upon you; hasten to me! Give ear to my voice when I call to you!" (Ps. 141:1). "Save me, God! The water is already up to my neck!" (Ps. 69:1 JB). Suffering prompted the psalmists to run to God because they knew he loved them, just like children run to their parents when they are frightened or hurt.

Of course, the mere fact these laments outnumber every other sort of prayer in the psalms doesn't prove the psalmists suffered often. Perhaps they knew long stretches of life that were relatively trouble free. Perhaps the psalms include so many laments simply because the psalmists prayed more when they were suffering. But I think there is more to it than that. After the first two psalms introduce the entire book,[7] David's first words in Psalm 3 are, "O LORD, how many are my foes!" This is the first of a string of five of David's laments.[8] In fact, thirty-nine laments mention David in their titles. Surely this is significant. God had sought out David as someone after his own heart (see 1 Sam. 13:14), but even being specially chosen by God didn't protect him from a great deal of suffering. For instance, he suffered resistance throughout his reign, prompting him to declare, "The righteous person faces *many* troubles" (Ps. 34:19 NLT). In fact, his troubles seem to have been the means by which God kept David's heart soft so that he would stay close to him.[9]

---

b. Perhaps grief (see Ps. 31:9) or loneliness (see Pss. 25:16; 102:6–7) or emotional exhaustion (see Pss. 6:6 NIV; 69:3 NLT).

Indeed, the author of Psalm 71 declared that God had made him "see troubles, many and bitter," which had taken him down into "the depths of the earth" (71:20 NIV). And Psalm 90 includes lines such as these:

> All our days pass away under your wrath;
>> we bring our years to an end like a sigh.
> The years of our life are seventy,
>> or even by reason of strength eighty;
> yet their span is but toil and trouble;
>> they are soon gone, and we fly away. (90:9–10)

Laments like these remind us that a life of faith is often puzzling or distressing. And yet we need to keep on praying, as our Lord made clear in a story meant to encourage us always to pray and never lose heart (see Luke 18:1–8). Slow, repeated, prayerful readings of these psalms make godly suffering less startling and thereby helps us catch our breath.

Breathing Lesson 2: Pray Properly

These psalms of lament also show us *how* to breathe. As acts of faith, they are little portraits of proper praying. Faithful praying has a rhythm that envelops our suffering in hopeful stories. Here are its three most crucial beats.

Remember (That Is, Inhale!)

Biblical faith involves our responses to God's initiatives.[10] For instance, after God created our first parents, he took the initiative in giving them a mandate and a commandment.[11] Later, he appeared to Abraham, telling him to leave his country, his relatives, and his father's household and go to a land that he would show him (see Gen. 12:1 with Acts 7:2–3). Still later, he heard Abraham's descendants groaning under Egyptian bondage and commissioned Moses to deliver them (see Ex. 2:23–3:10). Once they had become the nation of Israel, the Lord sought out David, commanding him to be a prince over his people (see 1 Sam. 13:13–14). In these and countless other cases, God took the initiative in caring for his Old Testament people, who were then to acknowledge what he was doing and respond appropriately.

Faithful lamenting is grounded in remembering what God has always done. The psalmists caught their breath by reminding themselves that their help always came from God. "If the LORD had not been my help, my soul would soon have lived in the land of silence" (Ps. 94:17). This reminded them of who God is:

> The king is not saved by his great army;
>> a warrior is not delivered by his great strength.
> The war horse is a false hope for salvation,
>> and by its great might it cannot rescue. . . .
> Our soul waits for the LORD;
>> he is our help and our shield. (Ps. 33:16–17, 20)

And this led them to pray that God would help them again:

> To you, O LORD, I call;
>> my rock, be not deaf to me,
> lest, if you be silent to me,
>> I become like those who go down to the pit.
> Hear the voice of my pleas for mercy,
>> when I cry to you for help. (Ps. 28:1–2)

The psalmists reminded themselves that God was the maker of heaven and earth:

> I lift up my eyes to the hills.
>> From where does my help come?
> My help comes from the LORD,
>> who made heaven and earth. (Ps. 121:1–2; cf. 124:1–3, 8)

Remembering he had spoken everything into existence, they inhaled the assurance that his plans could not be frustrated and he would accomplish all he intended, no matter what others planned (see Ps. 33:6–11). They remembered that he had frustrated Pharaoh and then helped them rout the nations occupying the promised land so it could be their dwelling place. These things proved his saving strength (see Ps. 80:8–11, 19). They proved nothing was too hard for him.[12]

When David felt threatened, he responded by reminding himself that all the days of his life were in God's hands (see Pss. 31:15 and 139:16 NIV). When he despaired because of his sin, he remembered God's unfailing love and abundant mercy (see Ps. 69, especially vv. 5–6, 13, 16, 19–20). When he couldn't understand why God did not immediately vanquish the wicked (see, e.g., Ps. 10:1–2), he recalled God's former wonderful deeds and thus reassured himself that "the LORD sits enthroned forever; he has established his throne for justice" (Ps. 9:7), which means God takes note of the trouble and grief the wicked cause in order finally to end their terror. And when another psalmist felt threatened in old age, he recalled God's care for him from before he was born as well as God's countless saving acts since. This made him confident God would bring him honor and comfort again.[13]

The psalmists summed up their trust in God in terms of knowing his name: "Those who know your name trust in you" (Ps. 9:10 NIV). "May the LORD answer you in the day of trouble! May the name of the God of Jacob protect you! . . . Some trust in chariots and some in horses, but we trust in the name of the LORD our God" (Ps. 20:1, 7). Knowing God's name means understanding him as he has revealed himself in his words and deeds.[14] It means remembering that his steadfast love "extends to the heavens" and his faithfulness "to the clouds," that his righteousness "is like the mountains of God" and his justice is "like the great deep" (Ps. 36:5–6; cf. 89:14). It also means remembering that "the LORD is great, and . . . above all gods" and, consequently:

Whatever the LORD pleases, he does,
  in heaven and on earth,
  in the seas and all deeps. (Ps. 135:6)

This God can save, has saved, and will continue to save (see Pss. 136:10–24; 36:6; 109:21; 130:7; 138:8; and 143:12). And indeed we, God's New Testament people, have been given yet another name, for a virgin bore a son who was called *Jesus* because he saves his people from their sins (see Matt. 1:18–23).[c]

---

c. *Jesus* transliterates the Hebrew name *Joshua*, which means "Yahweh saves." He is also called *Immanuel*, which means "God with us" (see Matt. 1:23).

In Psalm 91, we find the psalmist declaring his trust in his Lord:

> He who dwells in the shelter of the Most High
>   will abide in the shadow of the Almighty.
> I will say to the LORD, "My refuge and my fortress,
>   my God, in whom I trust." (91:1–2)

And then we hear God himself affirming the psalmist's faith:

> Because he holds fast to me in love, I will deliver him;
>   I will protect him, because he knows my name.
> When he calls to me, I will answer him;
>   I will be with him in trouble;
>   I will rescue him and honor him.
> With long life I will satisfy him
>   and show him my salvation. (91:14–16)

Breathing in such truths prompted the psalmists to breathe out their distress to God whenever they were troubled: "O God, save me by your name, and vindicate me by your might" (Ps. 54:1). "Spread your protection over them, [O God,] that those who love your name may rejoice in you." (Ps. 5:11 NIV; cf. Jer. 9:23–24).

The laments never merely vent the psalmists' feelings. They always address God as the one who has promised to deliver those who love him, know his name, and call upon him.

Pray Honestly and Thoroughly (In Other Words, Exhale!)

Some of the laments merely call God's attention to a troublesome situation, confident he will respond as promised:

> LORD, how many are my foes!
>   How many rise up against me!
> Many are saying of me,
>   "God will not deliver him."
> But you, LORD, are a shield around me,
>   my glory, the One who lifts my head high.

I call out to the LORD,
>   and he answers me from his holy mountain. (Ps. 3:1–4 NIV)

Some of them breathe out more desperate appeals:

Hear my prayer, O LORD;
>   let my cry come to you!
Do not hide your face from me
>   in the day of my distress!
Incline your ear to me;
>   answer me speedily in the day when I call! (Ps. 102:1–2)

Others, noting some apparent discrepancy between the psalmists' situations and God's promise, express some perplexity: "Why, O LORD, do you stand far away? Why do you hide yourself in times of trouble?" (Ps. 10:1). Others breathe out deeper perplexity:

Each day I beg for your help, O LORD;
>   I lift my hands to you for mercy.
Are your wonderful deeds of any use to the dead?
>   Do the dead rise up and praise you? . . .
O LORD, I cry out to you.
>   I will keep on pleading day by day.
O LORD, why do you reject me?
>   Why do you turn your face from me? (Ps. 88:9–10,
>   13–14 NLT)

Yet still others move from perplexity to frank complaint. For instance, at one point David felt overwhelmed by the treachery of a once-close friend and so addressed God like this:

God, hear my prayer,
>   do not hide from my petition,
give me a hearing, answer me,
>   I cannot rest for complaining.

I shudder at the enemy's shouts,
>   at the howling of the wicked;

they bring misery crashing down on me,
> and vent their fury on me.

My heart aches in my breast,
Death's terrors assail me,
fear and trembling descend on me,
> horror overwhelms me.

And I say,
"Oh for the wings of a dove
> to fly away and find rest."
How far I would take my flight,
> and make a new home in the desert! (Ps. 55:1–7 JB)

God had promised David rest from all his enemies, so David felt justified in complaining, even while he trusted God to hear him and respond appropriately:[15]

I . . . appeal to God
> and [the LORD] saves me;
evening, morning, noon,
> I complain, I groan;
> he will hear me calling.

His peace can ransom me
> from the war being waged on me.
How many are ranged against me!
> But God will hear me. (Ps. 55:16–17 JB)

He adds:

Sovereign from the first, he will humble them. . . .
> For my part, I put my trust in you. (Ps. 55:19, 23 JB; cf.
> > Pss. 64; 142)

A few of the laments even breathe out outright protest:

God, have you finally rejected us,
raging at the flock you used to pasture?

> Remember the people you long since made your own,
> your hereditary tribe whom you redeemed,
> and this Mount Zion where you came to live. . . .
>
> *Respect the covenant! We can bear no more. . . .*
> Do not let the hard-pressed retreat in confusion,
> give the poor and needy cause to praise your name. (Ps. 74:1–2,
>   20–21 JB)

All this honesty was appropriate because it arose from having breathed in God's promises. Realizing this helps us breathe.

These prayers are emotional. The psalmists didn't just *say* they were suffering; they sought words describing their distress. Their words help us feel their anguish, countering our tendency to think our suffering is unique. Even if we don't find our exact griefs in the psalms, we find anguish at least as deep.

The psalmists were particularly sensitive to shame and disgrace, so when they felt God had unjustifiably disgraced them, they protested:

> But you have rejected us and disgraced us. . . .
> You have made us the taunt of our neighbors,
>   the derision and scorn of those around us.
> You have made us a byword among the nations,
>   a laughingstock among the peoples. . . .
>
> All this has come upon us,
>   though we have not forgotten you,
>   and we have not been false to your covenant.
> Our heart has not turned back,
>   nor have our steps departed from your way. (Ps. 44:9, 13–14,
>   17–18)

This was so exasperating that these petitioners risked theological incorrectness in order to give breath to their true feelings: "Wake up, O Lord! Why do you sleep? Get up! Do not reject us forever" (Ps. 44:23 NLT; cf. 35:22–23).[16]

They dared such transparency because they knew that God knew what was festering in their hearts (see Pss. 44:21; 139:1–4; cf. Heb. 4:13). They knew they would damage their relationships with him by trying to hide the truth (see Ps. 32:1–6), so they spoke what they felt—and thus they coach us to keep calling on God, to keep addressing him, even if that means complaining or protesting. In short, we must keep breathing. This shows that biblical faith is not mere mindless acquiescence.[17] Read Psalms 44, 88, and 89, noting how bleakly each ends. These psalmists expressed their sorrows, perplexities, and complaints to God as honestly as they could.[18] Their faith inspired them to be remarkably free in baring their hearts to him. These laments—along with others scattered throughout the Old Testament—should encourage us to do the same.

Yet we are not only free to bare our hearts to God when we are suffering; we *need* to cry out to him. God promises to answer *when we call* (see Pss. 50:15; 91:15). As David learned, even well-intended silence can make things worse (see Ps. 39, especially vv. 1–3, 9–13). We need to be thorough and tell God all our troubles (see Ps. 142:1–2, 5–7 NLT).

The New Testament reiterates this. Paul reminded the severely persecuted Thessalonians that Christian suffering is common and then exhorted them to "pray without ceasing," presumably to keep Satan from unsettling them because of their suffering (see 1 Thess. 5:17, read in the light of 1:6; 2:14; and 3:1–5; cf. Rom. 12:12). James asked, "Is anyone among you suffering?" and then said, "Let him pray" (James 5:13).

Praying the laments helps us understand and cope with our own suffering. Praying Psalm 102 gave me words that articulated my own distress.[d] Once David made his initial plea for God to hear and answer him in Psalm 55, he breathed out his feelings in detail, thus modeling the advice he gave to others in verse 22: "Cast your burden on the LORD, and he will sustain you." Expressing our troubles to God helps us cast them more fully on him (cf. 1 Pet. 5:6–7).

Sometimes we must lament in order to work through our perplexities. When God revealed to Jeremiah his own family's plot against him,

---

d. See chap. 1, pp. 18–19.

Jeremiah lamented: "You are always righteous, LORD, when I bring a case before you. Yet I would speak with you about your justice: Why does the way of the wicked prosper? Why do all the faithless live at ease?" (Jer. 12:1 NIV with 11:18 and 12:6; cf. Hab. 1:13). At this point, Jeremiah wasn't doubting God's perfect righteousness, but he was puzzled how it worked in such cases. This prompted him to pray.[19]

At times the psalmists voiced more open-ended questions:

> Will the Lord spurn forever,
>   and never again be favorable?
> Has his steadfast love forever ceased?
>   Are his promises at an end for all time?
> Has God forgotten to be gracious?
>   Has he in anger shut up his compassion? (Ps. 77:7–9)

At other times they fired volleys of questions at God, probably implying that his apparent neglect was unbearable: "How long, LORD? Will you forget me forever? How long will you hide your face from me? How long must I wrestle with my thoughts and day after day have sorrow in my heart? How long will my enemy triumph over me? Look on me and answer, LORD my God" (Ps. 13:1–3 NIV).

The psalmists often needed imagery in order to express their feelings adequately. For instance, they often complained of being near death, portraying their distress in terms of their drowning (see Ps. 69:1, 14–15) or sinking in the mire (see Ps. 69:2, 14) or by having been cast into the depths of the earth, the grave, or the pit (see Pss. 88:3–6; 130:1). It seems it was only through using such language that they could begin expressing how suffocating their suffering felt. They conveyed their feeling of being pressed or pursued to the point of exhaustion by likening their enemies' attempts to destroy them to hiding traps, setting nets, and digging pits (see Pss. 142:3; 35:7; 57:6). This threatened their futures and made their deaths seem imminent. Experiences like these weren't fully expressible in words, but they needed to try to express them nonetheless.[20]

Remember Again (Inhale Again!)

When suffering overwhelms us, it is easy to despair. Yet amazingly, with only one possible exception (see Ps. 88), the psalmists were never so overwhelmed by their suffering as to lose all hope.[21] This is because after they breathed out their troubles to God, they breathed in again. They reminded themselves of God's character, his promises, his previous wondrous acts for Israel, and his record of individualized care. By focusing on facts that made them confident their God would ultimately put things right, they countered their feelings with history and theological truth. Faithful lamenting begins and ends with remembering.

We can watch David breathing in Psalm 22. He first exhaled with the plaintive cry,

My God, my God, why have you forsaken me?
    Why are you so far from saving me, from the words of my
        groaning?
O my God, I cry by day, but you do not answer,
    and by night, but I find no rest. (22:1–2)

Then he inhaled by recalling God's holiness and his previous deliverance of Israel:

Yet, Holy One, you
who make your home in the praises of Israel,
in you our fathers put their trust,
they trusted and you rescued them;
they called to you for help and they were saved,
they never trusted you in vain. (22:3–5 JB)

He then exhaled again, conveying some of the existential horror of his situation by means of an arresting image—

Yet here am I, now more worm than man,
scorn of mankind, jest of the people,
all who see me jeer at me,
they toss their heads and sneer,

"He relied on [the LORD], let [the LORD] save him!
If [the LORD] is his friend, let Him rescue him!" (22:6–8 JB)[22]

—only to inhale the history of God's goodness to him, which then became the basis of a plea:

> Yet you are he who took me from the womb;
>> you made me trust you at my mother's breasts.
> On you was I cast from my birth,
>> and from my mother's womb you have been my God.
> Be not far from me,
>> for trouble is near,
>> and there is none to help. (22:9–11)

He then exhaled once more, breathing out this vivid raft of images that liken his enemies to dangerous, wild animals and flesh out his psychosomatic reactions with similes of physical dissipation and degradation:

> My enemies surround me like a herd of bulls;
>> fierce bulls of Bashan have hemmed me in!
> Like lions they open their jaws against me,
>> roaring and tearing into their prey.
> My life is poured out like water,
>> and all my bones are out of joint.
> My heart is like wax,
>> melting within me.
> My strength has dried up like sunbaked clay.
>> My tongue sticks to the roof of my mouth.
>> You have laid me in the dust and left me for dead.
> My enemies surround me like a pack of dogs;
>> an evil gang closes in on me.
>> They have pierced my hands and feet.
> I can count all my bones.
>> My enemies stare at me and gloat. (22:12–17 NLT)

These images then formed the content of his primary plea:

But you, LORD, be not far from me.
> You are my strength; come quickly to help me.
Deliver me from the sword,
> my precious life from the power of the dogs.
Rescue me from the mouth of the lions;
> save me from the horns of the wild oxen. (22:19–21 NIV)

Then, right in the midst of all this careful breathing, David went from pleading to vowing to praise God and then to actually praising him:

I will tell of your name to my brothers;
> in the midst of the congregation I will praise you:
You who fear the LORD, praise him!
All you offspring of Jacob, glorify him,
> and stand in awe of him, all you offspring of Israel!
For he has not despised or abhorred
> the affliction of the afflicted,
and he has not hidden his face from him,
> but has heard, when he cried to him. (22:22–24)

David's perspective had changed abruptly. For the rest of the psalm, he took his pleas as answered, focusing on praising God for answering them. As he did so, his sense of deliverance through God's overruling providence became so strong that it broadened out into a prediction:

All the ends of the earth shall remember
> and turn to the LORD,
and all the families of the nations
> shall worship before you.
For kingship belongs to the LORD,
> and he rules over the nations. (22:27–28)

Indeed, David declared, all humankind would bow before the Lord, and his righteousness would be proclaimed to a people yet unborn (see 22:29–31).

Psalm 22 is extraordinary in many ways, but it is quite ordinary in its movement from complaint through plea to confident praise. This is standard with the Psalms' individual laments.[23] At some point each psalmist quit lamenting and complaining, quit asking and pleading, and began praising. This change was often marked by words such as "Yet you" or "But you" or even in some contexts "But I." These words signaled a shift in the psalmist's perspective from doubt and alarm to trust and peace.[24] The immediate cause of the psalmists' new confidence is usually unclear, although occasionally they stated what prompted it. Once, halfway through a psalm and right before expressing his confidence, David quoted God as having spoken: "'Because the poor are plundered, because the needy groan, I will now arise,' says the Lord; 'I will place him in the safety for which he longs'" (Ps. 12:5). Usually, however, the psalmists began hoping again simply through faithfully remembering their grounds for hope. In any case, they began trusting God again.

FINAL LESSONS

So what do these psalms finally teach us?

First, their frequency assures us that David and the other psalmists regularly found God willing to hear and respond to their complaints and pleas. Suffering people learn not to waste their breath complaining to imaginary persons or to those who won't listen or respond. Of course, God's response was not always immediate. As David counseled:

> Commit your way to the Lord;
>   trust in him, and he will act. . . .
> Be still before the Lord *and wait patiently for him.* (Ps. 37:5, 7)

David had learned that God knows the days of his people and that he will not let them ultimately be put to shame (see Ps. 37:18–19). Knowing this, he confessed: "Praise is due to you, O God, in Zion, and to you shall vows be performed. O you who hear prayer, to you shall all flesh come" (Ps. 65:1–2; cf. Ps. 40:1–3).

Second, the constant use of these psalms as part of the Christian church's prayer life testifies that God has regularly and unmistakably met his suffering saints throughout the centuries as they have made these laments their own.[25]

Third, the all but invariable arc from complaint through plea to confident praise should encourage us always to be looking beyond our suffering. David had learned over time that God would always rescue him because God had heard his pleas for mercy again and again:

> Blessed be the LORD,
>> for he has wondrously shown his steadfast love to me. . . .
> I had said in my alarm,
>> "I am cut off from your sight."
> But you heard the voice of my pleas for mercy
>> when I cried to you for help.
> Love the LORD, all you his saints!
>> The LORD preserves the faithful. . . .
> Be strong, and let your heart take courage,
>> all you who wait for the LORD! (Ps. 31:21–24)

Because God faithfully delivered them, the psalmists loved him and resolved to call on him as long as they lived:

> I love the LORD, for he heard my voice;
>> he heard my cry for mercy.
> Because he turned his ear to me,
>> I will call on him as long as I live. . . .
> For you, LORD, have delivered me from death,
>> my eyes from tears,
>> my feet from stumbling. (Ps. 116:1–2, 8 NIV; cf. 71:20–22)

This led them to pray frankly and yet faithfully: "I believed, even when I spoke: 'I am greatly afflicted'" (Ps. 116:10). As we pattern our prayers on these psalms and then find that God hears us, we learn the same lesson.

Finally, their sheer brevity helps. As we are about to see, we must read four chapters in the book of Ruth and forty-one chapters of Job before learning of Naomi's and Job's relief. We will see Jeremiah regain his faith and hope halfway through his book, although he was never free of suffering. Yet in the psalms, relief usually comes in less than a page. Of course, relief doesn't usually come in a day, and nothing can guarantee that we won't panic or despair in our suffering. Yet praying these laments, and thus experiencing through them the inevitable transition from complaint through plea to confident praise, can help us breathe. They are meant to assure us that, no matter how bad things currently seem, God is with us.

So it must have been for our Lord when, as he hung on the cross, he took the opening cry of Psalm 22 upon his lips (see Matt. 27:46). Surely he would have been conscious, to a degree unmatched by any of us, of that psalm's arc. He would have applied each part to himself, including its final triumphant predictions. This helped him to breathe and thus endure unprecedented and forever unparalleled suffering so that he might know the joy that lay ahead (see Heb. 12:2). No doubt a lifetime in the psalms had taught him, as it should teach us, how to choose faithfulness and hopefulness again and again.

Learning these lessons can help us breathe when we are suffering. They help us keep true perspective.

THE REST OF THEIR STORIES

God's Steadfast Love for Naomi, Job, and Jeremiah

The LORD descended in the cloud and stood with [Moses] . . .
and proclaimed [his] name. . . .
"The LORD, the LORD, a God merciful and gracious,
slow to anger, and abounding in steadfast love and faithfulness,
keeping steadfast love for thousands,
forgiving iniquity and transgression and sin."

Exodus 34:5–7

So Boaz took Ruth and she became his wife.
When he made love to her, the LORD enabled her to conceive,
and she gave birth to a son.
The women said to Naomi:
"Praise be to the LORD, who this day has not
left you without a guardian-redeemer.
May he become famous throughout Israel! He will renew your life
and sustain you in your old age." . . .
Then Naomi took the child in her arms and cared for him.
The women living there said, "Naomi has a son!"
And they named him Obed.
He was the father of Jesse, the father of David.

Ruth 4:13–17 (NIV)

Then Job replied to the LORD:
"I know that you can do all things;
no purpose of yours can be thwarted.
You asked, 'Who is this that obscures my plans without knowledge?'
Surely I spoke of things I did not understand,
things too wonderful for me to know.
You said, 'Listen now, and I will speak;
I will question you, and you shall answer me.'
My ears had heard of you but now my eyes have seen you.
Therefore I despise myself and repent in dust and ashes."

Job 42:1–6 (NIV)

I am the man who has seen affliction. . . .
[The LORD] has driven and brought me into
darkness without any light. . . .
He has besieged and enveloped me with
bitterness and tribulation. . . .
My soul is bereft of peace; I have forgotten what happiness is;
so I say, "My endurance has perished;
so has my hope from the LORD." . . .
But this I call to mind, and therefore I have hope: . . .
The Lord will not cast off forever,
but, though he cause grief, he will have compassion
according to the abundance of his steadfast love;
for he does not [willingly] afflict . . . or grieve the children of men.

Lamentations 3:1–2, 5, 17–18, 21, 31–33

Suffering challenges our settled perspectives, making us question their truth. This can be deeply disorienting, as we saw in chapter 1. Graham's parents' insistent, unanswered questions about God's apparent indifference to his struggle and death have left them profoundly disillusioned, making it extremely difficult for them to find a hopeful and thus livable Christian perspective. My seasons of disorienting perplexity involved nothing as horrible, so my loss of perspective was never as great. In the storm on the Mediterranean Sea, Paul's companions experienced another kind of disorientation. Having lost all sense of where they were, they feared what the wind and waves would do to their ship and finally lost all hope that they would live.

STORIES

We orient ourselves by means of stories.[a] Our personal stories locate us in time and space. The more comprehensive ones start in the relatively distant past: "I was born in Warren, Ohio, in 1950, and lived there until I was seven. We then moved to Seattle, where my father was an engineer at Boeing. When I was seventeen I suffered a paralyzing accident." They stretch through the present: "I decided last evening that when I got up this morning, I would spend all day working on this chapter, which I'm now doing." And they extend into the future: "I hope to have this book finished this month." Each part can be made more specific: "I started late this morning, around seven o'clock. Since then, my writing has been interrupted twice. But I'm still encouraged by the progress I seem to be making."

Such stories are the stuff of everyday human life. They are so common that we often don't realize when we are living one. Suppose, for instance, it's early morning. You feel a twinge of thirst. You think about how you want to satisfy it. You decide you'd like a glass of orange juice. So you get up, walk to the kitchen, get a glass out of the cupboard, put it on the counter, walk over to the refrigerator, open its door, spot the orange juice carton, reach for it, pull it out of the fridge, walk back to the counter, shake the carton, open it, pour some juice in your glass, close the carton, put it back in the fridge, close the door, turn back to the counter, pick up your glass, and (finally!) take your first sip. Congratulations! You've just finished a very short story.

---

a. See my preliminary remarks about stories near the end of chap. 1, pp. 20–21.

We also tend to embrace some big, general story that tells us what human life means. Christians embrace the Christian story, situating their personal stories within it and thus orienting themselves according to its overall storyline. Scripture opens with two chapters recounting creation and closes with two more foretelling a consummation that will complete everything. So *creation* and *consummation* are the Christian storyline's bookends, its beginning and end. They portray paradises of divinely ordered blessedness yielding unalloyed pleasures to those inhabiting them.

In between, we find *rebellion* and *redemption*. Our first parents forfeited creation's initial blessedness when they rebelled against God's command not to eat the forbidden fruit, thereby plunging the whole world into sin, suffering, and death. Much later, our Lord became incarnate so he could redeem us from sin. We now hope for his return, which will usher us into the consummation of his everlasting presence and deliver us from all suffering.[1] Much more on these themes in my later volumes.

Orienting ourselves by stories involves using their storylines to put our lives in proper perspective. This gives us meaning and purpose. Deciding to go to the kitchen to get a glass of orange juice gives you a purpose that means you must now engage in a series of acts to fulfill that purpose. This includes getting up, walking to the kitchen, getting out a glass, opening the fridge, spotting the orange juice carton, pouring out some juice, and lifting the glass to your lips. Each act derives its meaning from its part in helping you fulfill your purpose. You keep it all in perspective by being aware of where you are in the series that began with deciding to go to the kitchen to have a glass of orange juice and will end when you're drinking it. In other words, you only know where you are and what you are doing in terms of a storyline that stretches from a beginning to an end.

Deciding to go to the kitchen involves having specific beliefs and hopes—such as believing you will get there and hoping to find orange juice in the refrigerator. But suppose that before you get up, you remember there isn't any orange juice. Then you won't go to the kitchen hoping to get some. Or suppose that on your way you encounter water dripping from the hallway ceiling. Stopping to investigate will interrupt your story. It may even change it into a different story that doesn't end with your drinking orange juice in the kitchen.

With longer, less familiar stories, our awareness of our place in the storyline and what we should expect often needs to be made more explicit. Longer storylines increase the chances that something will prevent us from reaching their ends. This is especially true with our lives' more important stories. Suppose a high schooler decides to embrace the storyline that is meant to end in her becoming a primary-care physician. A lot can disrupt that story. She may simply change her mind, deciding she would rather be a research biologist. Or she may take a trip that exposes her to a new culture and makes her want to live an entirely different kind of life. She could (like me) suffer a paralyzing accident that would alter her plans.

Her embracing that storyline may also include her having unrealistic expectations that invite disillusionment or disorientation. For instance, she needs to consider the costs involved in her getting from its beginning to its end. This includes her needing to understand the educational commitments she must make. Suppose she never considers the stiffer competition she will face in college, requiring her to study much harder. The shock of discovering this and then facing the unexpected prospect of so much hard work and so little play may disillusion her, prompting her to reconsider her high school decision. Her progress to her goal could also be interrupted by her unexpectedly running out of funds, by her getting married and having a baby, or by something causing her to become severely depressed.

Because the Christian story starts with creation and stretches forward into the consummation of everlasting life, no storyline can be longer or more significant. Embracing the Christian storyline involves taking its perspective as giving our entire lives their overall meaning and purpose.

THE FULL CHRISTIAN STORY

As with other important stories, misleading expectations or unexpected events involving the Christian storyline can trigger disillusionment or disorientation. For instance, Graham's parents were orienting themselves by a widespread yet false storyline about the Christian life. It portrayed their all-powerful, all-knowing heavenly Father as unwilling to let one of his children suffer and die in the way Graham did, especially if they petitioned him with earnest, believing prayer. Graham's death has then left them profoundly disillusioned. My own disorientations involved my belief that God causes all things to work together for good for those who love him (see Rom. 8:28) and yet being unable to believe that some unexpected and very disturbing events in my life could work together for good. I couldn't find a perspective on them that made good sense to me. So I couldn't understand how my experience could be part of what I understood to be the story I was in.

In situations like these, the psalmists' frank complaints and desperate pleas can help us embrace the full Christian story. As R. W. L. Moberly has said, the "predominance of laments at the very heart of Israel's prayers means that the problems that give rise to lament are not something marginal or unusual but . . . are central in the life of faith. . . . *They show that the experience of anguish and puzzlement . . . is intrinsic to the very nature of faith.*"[2]

It is also intrinsic to the nature of biblical faith to believe that the Lord is always unremittingly *pursuing* his saints with his *chesed*[b]—that is, his *steadfast love, kindness, and faithfulness*. David emphasized this in Psalm 23. In declaring that the Lord was his shepherd and that he therefore had all that he needed (see Ps. 23:1 NLT), he was in effect already declaring what he concluded in its last verse—that "only goodness and steadfast love shall pursue me all the days of my life" (23:6a JPS) and that, consequently, when all was said and done, he would "dwell in the house of the LORD forever" (23:6b).[3] Yet, as David's laments show, we must learn to adjust our expectations about what the Lord's pursuit of us with his *chesed* entails, since Scripture shows that God's *chesed* is not always manifested in obvious and easily understandable ways.

Chesed, Daniel Block writes, "is one of those Hebrew words whose meaning cannot be captured in one English word." It "wraps up in itself

---

b. The introductory consonant is pronounced as the *ch* in Bach. Most Hebrew words emphasize the last syllable but not this one. So *chesed* is pronounced CHE-*sed*. The ESV almost always translates *chesed* as "steadfast love" or "kindness," while other versions translate it as "love," "unfailing love," "faithful love," "faithfulness," or "kindness."

an entire cluster of concepts, all the positive attributes of God—[his] love, mercy, grace, kindness, goodness, benevolence, loyalty, [and] covenant faithfulness."[4] It is the sort of love of God and neighbor that moves one person to act unselfishly for another's benefit. This steadfast, kind, loyal, and merciful loving concern for others is basic to God's character, being emblematic of all he is. God himself reiterated it as the central feature of his name in reassuring Moses that in spite of the Israelites' flagrant sin in worshiping the golden calf, he would still go with them to the promised land:[c]

> The LORD descended in the cloud and stood with [Moses] there, and proclaimed [his] name. . . . The LORD passed before him and proclaimed, "The LORD, the LORD, a God merciful and gracious, slow to anger, and abounding in steadfast love [*chesed*] and faithfulness, keeping steadfast love [*chesed*] for thousands, forgiving iniquity and transgression and sin, but who will by no means clear the guilty, visiting the iniquity of the fathers on the children and the children's children, to the third and the fourth generation." (Ex. 34:5–7; see also Ex. 20:6 and Deut. 5:10)

God's *chesed*, as the basic feature of his name or character, is emphasized throughout the Old Testament (see, e.g., Num. 14:17–19; Neh. 9:16–21; Jonah 4:2). It is mentioned a total of 245 times, with 127 instances in the Psalms, where, as we have already seen, the psalmists summed up their trust in God in terms of knowing his name.[d] When it appears in psalms of thanksgiving and praise, it reminds us of God's settled character, of his constant and indeed everlasting goodness (see Pss. 118; 136; 145).[5] When it appears in the laments, it shows us that recalling their Lord's steadfast love and kindness when they were suffering was key to the psalmists' maintaining their faith.

For instance, in Psalm 86 David invoked God's *chesed* three times (see 86:5, 13, 15). As Kidner notes, Psalm 86 is "a lonely prayer"—David

---

c. In Scripture, names often reveal the nature or character of the person named. At Ex. 34:5–7, God revealed what his name means in response to Moses having prayed at Ex. 33:13 that the Lord would show him his ways (cf. Ps. 103:7–11).

d. See chap. 3, p. 48.

was alone with his enemies, with no friends or allies in sight. This lament has a very simple structure: there are opening and closing pleas (see 86:1–7, 14–17), interrupted "by a deliberate act of praise—*deliberate*," Kidner emphasizes, "because the final verses reveal no abatement of the pressure, and no sign, as yet, of an answer."[6] David's appeal to God's *chesed* was integral to his pleas for God to save him. The last appeal occurred in the middle of his most desperate and specific plea. In verse 14 he stated that a band of proud, ruthless, and godless men were seeking to kill him. But then in verse 15 he quoted Exodus 34:6, pleading, "But you, O Lord, are a God *merciful and gracious, slow to anger and abounding in steadfast love and faithfulness.*" This appeal to God's character then grounded David's final plea:

> Turn to me and be gracious to me;
>> give your strength to your servant,
>> and save the son of your maidservant.
> Show me a sign of your favor,
>> that those who hate me may see and be put to shame
>> because you, LORD, have helped me and comforted me.
> (Ps. 86:16–17)

What God had revealed about himself in Exodus 34, combined with David's recollection in this psalm of God's rescues in the past, led him to expect and believe—in spite of all appearances to the contrary—that God had not abandoned him and would ultimately deliver him again.

As D. A. Baer and R. P. Gordon observe, the biblical authors understand that "life is fragile." They are acutely aware that our lives are beset by many kinds of threats, including "the calamities of nature, the hostility of enemies, and the weakness of self." And, consequently, they "plead for God to save them by his [*chesed*]," recognizing that "God's [*chesed*] is their only hedge against disaster." The Psalms in particular, Baer and Gordon stress, "are full of this motif." And yet rarely

> is the eventual salvation that God's [*chesed*] provides seen to eradicate the anxiety of the endangered while they await deliverance. . . .

This dynamic, whereby one must discover God's [*chesed*] all over again at each new crisis, seems central to God's ways with humankind as the biblical authors present it. While one recounts God's [*chesed*] to one's fellows in the hope that they will learn to trust in it when distress comes upon them, the pain and pathos of waiting are never fully displaced.[7]

What is happening to us may perplex us, especially if we are Christians. Yet we should see our suffering as part of ordinary Christian experience (see 1 Pet. 1:3–7; 4:12–19).

Yet God's *chesed* does indeed guarantee that he is being loving to us and that his kindness will become clear to us in the end. In proclaiming to Moses his name as "The LORD, . . . a God merciful and gracious, slow to anger, and abounding in [*chesed*] and faithfulness," God, who cannot lie, was vowing never to abandon his people (see Heb. 6:18). The Hebrew word translated as "abounding" comes from a verbal root that denotes the rapid growth or multiplication of something—so for God to declare that he *abounds* in *chesed* means that it is his character to be always overflowing in great quantities of steadfast love and faithfulness to his people, no matter how it may seem. Threats and calamities may dog us during our earthly lives, but "*only* goodness and steadfast love shall pursue [us] all the days of [our lives]," just as David said (Ps. 23:6 JPS). Or as he put it elsewhere:

> Sing praises to the LORD, O you his saints,
>   and give thanks to his holy name.
> For his anger is but for a moment,
>   and his favor is for a lifetime.
> Weeping may tarry for the night,
>   but joy comes with the morning. (Ps. 30:4–5)

Only the Lord's steadfast love "endures forever" (Ps. 138:8).

David coupled his repeated invocations of God's *chesed* in Psalm 86 with the declaration that no one can rival God or oppose his wondrous, saving acts (see 86:8–10). He took God's abounding *chesed* for him to be the one absolutely unvarying constant of his life, and he took God's power to accomplish all that his *chesed* intended to be unstoppable. These two articles of faith led him to declare, *even before he had experienced it*, that God had helped, comforted, and delivered him (see 86:13, 17).[e]

It is by breathing in these words that God has breathed out for us that we learn to embrace the full Christian story. They remind us who God is and what he does and *does not* promise. And thus they help us to avoid disillusionment and disorientation by enabling us to hope more realistically.

Yet in our suffering, we may find the psalmists' hopeful arc from complaint through plea to confident praise to be almost unbelievable. We may lose the true biblical perspective and become disillusioned or disoriented in our faith. So here we need to finish Naomi's, Job's, and Jeremiah's stories. Their stories show that God's steadfast love and invincible power may be working for us, even when we lack eyes to see or hearts to welcome God's providential pathway to our good.

THE REST OF THEIR STORIES

We saw in chapter 2 how Naomi, Job, and Jeremiah lost perspective when they were suffering profoundly. They became unsure what kind of stories they were in. Even worse, they then lost hope and began believing false stories. Yet Scripture shows they were mistaking appearances for reality, for when their full stories are told and we become aware of all that was said and done, we see that God had been working all along to bless and keep them.

Naomi's Full Story: God Restores Her Life's Pleasantness

The book of Ruth highlights the immense contrast between how things may appear in the midst of great suffering and how we may see them as we emerge from it. Throughout the time covered in its first chapter,

---

e. The verb tenses in these two verses can be interpreted in more than one way, but I think they are best interpreted as being what grammarians call the *prophetic perfect*, which means that they express "the certainty of future events as though they were already complete" (Derek Kidner, *Psalms 73–150* [London: Inter-Varsity Press, 1975], 313).

Naomi felt that what was happening to her was so irreversibly bad that her name needed to be changed from Pleasant to Bitter. Yet its final chapter reveals that Naomi's hopelessness in the midst of her suffering was no measure of God's ability to work out everything for her good. When Naomi took Ruth's infant, Obed, into her arms at the story's end, her life was being restored by the same God who had made it so bitter. It was no irony to call her "Pleasant" again.

The dialogues between Naomi and the women of Bethlehem highlight this. In chapter 1 she declared to them, "Do not call me Naomi" (meaning *pleasant*); "call me Mara" (meaning *bitter*), "for the Almighty has dealt very bitterly with me. I went away full, and the LORD has brought me back empty. Why call me Naomi, when the LORD has testified against me and the Almighty has brought calamity upon me?" (1:20–21).[8] Having lost husband and sons, her life was decimated by death and emptiness. Yet when Obed was born and Naomi took him into her arms, the prospect of her life becoming pleasant again was reestablished, leading those women to exclaim that he would restore Naomi's life and care for her in her old age. Moreover, they noted, she was already experiencing the great pleasure of Ruth's love: "For . . . your daughter-in-law . . . loves you and has been better to you than seven sons!" (4:15 NLT).[9]

God's interventions in restoring Naomi's life frame the story. Chapter 1 states that he ended Israel's famine, prompting Naomi to rise, leave Moab, and take to the road leading back to Judah (see 1:6–7). And thus began, although she didn't yet know it, the story of her restoration. His intervention is not mentioned again until we read, "The LORD gave [the previously barren Ruth] conception, and she bore a son" (4:13). So God's "gracious provision of fruitfulness for 'field'" in chapter 1 "and 'womb'" in chapter 4 open and close the story of the Lord's *chesed* to Naomi.[10]

In between, he accomplished his *chesed* through his people's *chesed*. The loyalty, steadfast love, and kindness of Naomi, Ruth, and Boaz for each other animate the story.[11] Each knew it was not all about them. Even in the depths of her grief and hopelessness, Naomi showed *chesed* toward her daughters-in-law, urging them to return to their mothers' households because she felt that would be better for them (see 1:8–13, 15). Ruth's loyal and loving reply exemplified her *chesed*:

> Don't ask me to leave you and turn back. Wherever you go, I will go; wherever you live, I will live. Your people will be my people, and your God will be my God. Wherever you die, I will die, and there I will be buried. May the LORD punish me severely if I allow anything but death to separate us! (1:16–17 NLT)

And from the very start, Boaz cared for Ruth as part of his being loyal, loving, and kind to his kinswoman Naomi (see 2:1, 5–6, 8–16).[12]

These saints are never portrayed as praying for themselves, which shows that those who participate in God's *chesed* often think more about others than they do about themselves.[13] Their *chesed* appears primarily in their actions. For instance, Ruth doesn't talk much. She just *does* what is loving—among other things, demonstrating her *chesed* for Naomi in marrying Boaz rather than preferring someone younger.[14] Yet God honors those who practice *chesed* and repays their kindness to others with kindness to them. Boaz's and Ruth's *chesed* brought them blessings (see 3:9–10; 4:11–12) and Naomi's selfless, steadfast love for Ruth became the vehicle for her own restoration.[15] Likewise, when we are suffering profoundly, it is important to know that it is often only as we concentrate on relieving the suffering of others that we ourselves find orientation and relief.

This all gets nicely wrapped up in a crucial verbal *inclusio* that highlights God's providential care. An *inclusio* is a literary device—in this case, the repetition of a word—that puts bookends on the beginning and end of some meaningful piece of text. In chapter 1 Naomi said, "Do not call me Naomi; call me Mara, for the Almighty has dealt very bitterly with me. I went away full, and the LORD has *brought me back* empty" (1:20–21). Then in chapter 4 the Bethlehem women exclaimed that Obed would be "a restorer of life and a nourisher of [Naomi's] old age" (4:15). The phrase "restorer of life" translates literally as "he who causes life *to come back*." In each case the words I have italicized translate the Hebrew word *shuv*, which thus forms the *inclusio*. Since God gave Ruth conception and thus ultimately provided the child who was restoring Naomi's life, both Naomi's desolation and her restoration are attributed to God.

And so Naomi was right to take God as having ordained her suffering even if she was wrong to think it was so terrible that not even he could make her life pleasant again. And from our New Testament perspective we can now see that God intended Naomi's suffering to serve a far greater purpose than anything she could know in her lifetime. He was providentially accomplishing far more than anyone in the book of Ruth could ever have asked or imagined. For out of Naomi's desperate plight God brought Obed, who fathered Jesse, who fathered David, the great forefather of our Lord. So here is our first instance of the truth that "whatever was written in former days was written for our instruction, that through endurance and through the encouragement of the Scriptures we might have hope" (Rom. 15:4). Naomi's full story is not all about Naomi. It is not even (as perhaps the author of the book of Ruth thought) all about David. It is ultimately about God's providential provision of our Lord, which came about through Naomi's suffering.

Job Comfortably at Home Again

The book of Ruth shows that while Naomi temporarily lost hope that God would be good to her, she didn't lose hope altogether—or at least not for long. Her instructions to Ruth in chapters 2 and 3 show that she had begun to harbor hope again, at least for Ruth.[16] Job's disorientation and despair ran deeper. Although Job's first two chapters reveal that God's great regard for Job's righteousness accounted for Job's miseries, Job himself didn't know this—and, in fact, he couldn't have known it if God's purposes were to be accomplished. Yet as those miseries grew, Job came to believe God was being wrathful to him, hated him, and had even—figuratively speaking—gnashed his teeth at him (see Job 16:9; cf. 19:11 and 30:21). With one remarkable exception,[f] Job's prolonged suffering seems

---

f. "Though he slay me, I will hope in him; yet I will argue my ways to his face" (13:15). Job may have been expressing some sort of eschatological hope in a few other passages (see, e.g., 19:23–29),

to have regularly obscured his horizon of hope. In fact, his very poignant expressions of dashed hopes and personal hopelessness outnumber his expressions of hopefulness by at least eight to one. At one point, his suffering led him to lament that his days were "swifter than a weaver's shuttle and [came] to their end without hope," which then led him to the utterly despairing conclusion that his eye would *"never again* see good" (7:6–7).

Why did Job despair so deeply? Partly because of his social situation. Naomi's grief was always eased by human kindness. Ruth declared her irrevocable love and loyalty to Naomi as they paused on the road leading back to Bethlehem, and no hint of censure taints the welcome the women of Bethlehem gave her, despite the fact that Naomi and her family had forsaken Bethlehem during a famine and she was returning with a Moabite widow. Boaz's generosity to Ruth for Naomi's sake included his positive response to Ruth's advances toward him at night on the threshing floor (see Ruth 3:1–14). Later, as he finalized his plans to marry her, the onlookers prayed that God would bless the previously barren Ruth with offspring (see 4:9–12).

Contrast Job's situation. After his children died, he was afflicted with sores so loathsome that people shunned him.[17] He headed out of the city to sit on an ash heap, where he scraped his sores with pieces of broken pottery. His wife urged him to curse God and die (see Job 2:8–9). His spirits would have lifted when his three friends arrived, who at first responded appropriately (see 2:11–13). But they soon were offended by his words of grief and confusion and presumed his suffering was punishment for sin. They then drove their perspective home mercilessly.[18]

Job's first exchange with his friends made him feel he needed to warn them that they were treading on dangerous ground, ground that involved their withholding *chesed* from him: "Anyone who withholds kindness [*chesed*] from a friend forsakes the fear of the Almighty. But [you] . . . are as undependable as intermittent streams, as the streams that overflow when darkened by thawing ice and swollen with melting snow, but that stop flowing in the dry season, and in the heat vanish

---

but nowhere else as clearly as in this passage. (Merriam-Webster defines *eschatological* as "of, relating to, or dealing with the end of the world or the ultimate destiny of humankind," s.v. "eschatological," https://www.merriam-webster.com/dictionary/eschatological.)

from their channels" (6:14–17 NIV). He likened his seeking comfort from them to desert caravans that would confidently turn off from their routes seeking water, only to find none and then perish in the wastelands. "Now you too have proved to be of no help; you see something dreadful and are afraid" (6:21 NIV).

It seems that Job and his three friends had pledged to support each other through thick and thin, so Job expected their kindness and sympathy. Finding only condemnation aggravated his grief.[19]

Job's grief was deepened by his friends' demand for explanation. If they could explain his suffering, then they might be able to reassure themselves that they wouldn't suffer similarly. They began by assuming that an individual's sin is always the cause of his or her suffering and then concluded that Job's suffering was caused by hidden but egregious sin. They needed to acknowledge that someone's suffering may have nothing to do with that person's sin (see Eccles. 7:15; John 9:1–3) and, indeed, that God may ordain a saint's suffering for no discernible reason (see Job 2:3; 9:17).

Job increased his suffering by his own demand to know why the God whom he had always worshiped and obeyed was treating him so harshly:

> I loathe my life;
> I will give free utterance to my complaint;
>   I will speak in the bitterness of my soul.
> I will say to God, Do not condemn me;
>   let me know why you contend against me.
> Does it seem good to you to oppress,
>   to despise the work of your hands
>   and favor the designs of the wicked? (10:1–3)

Snatching at an explanation, he jumped to the conclusion that "God has wronged me" (19:6 NIV).[g] This led God to manifest his displeasure by appearing in a whirlwind to challenge Job: "Who is this that questions my wisdom with such ignorant words? Brace yourself like a man, because I have some questions for you, and you must answer them"

---

g. Ironically, Job's hasty condemnation of God was as uncharitable as his three friends' hasty condemnation of him.

(38:2–3 NLT). Job thought he understood God's ways (see 38:1–40:2). He thought he was seeing everything more or less whole and complete, when in fact his knowledge even of his own story was only fragmentary. God's questions helped him realize this: Where was Job at creation? Was he with God as God laid the earth's foundation? Did he know who marked off the earth's dimensions or who kept the sea within its proper boundaries as it burst into existence? Was he sovereign over the morning? Had he seen the gates of death? Could he control the rain? Did he hunt with the lions or provide the raven its prey? Did he give the warhorse its courage and strength? (see Job 38–39).

God closed these questions with one more: "Will the one who contends with the Almighty correct him? Let him who accuses God answer him!" (40:2 NIV). Awed by God's appearance in the whirlwind and convinced now of his ignorance, Job replied: "I am nothing—how could I ever find the answers? I will cover my mouth with my hand. I have said too much already. I have nothing more to say" (40:4–5 NLT). But the whirlwind continued and God persisted: "Would you discredit my justice? Would you condemn me to justify yourself?" (40:8 NIV).

These words may have been provoked by Job's final speech, where it seems he was so convinced that he was right that he could force God to vindicate him:

> Oh, that I had one to hear my case:
> > here is my signature: let the Almighty answer me!
> Let my accuser write out his indictment!
> Surely, I should wear it on my shoulder
> > or put it on me like a diadem;
> Of all my steps I should give him an account;
> > like a prince I should present myself before him.
> > > (31:35–37 NAB)

Job insisted that, given the opportunity, he would approach God with his head held high, sure of his authority and the rightness of his cause. He surrounded this bold declaration with a series of self-imprecatory curses affirming his utter moral purity (see 31:1–34, 38–40).[20]

We know from the book's prologue that Job was indeed "a blameless and upright man" who feared God and turned away from evil (2:3; cf. 1:1, 8). So he wasn't wrong to insist on his innocence. But he was wrong to think he could appear regally before God and successfully contend against him. So God challenged Job's assumption that he could force God to vindicate him:

> Have you an arm like God,
>   and can you thunder with a voice like his?
> Adorn yourself with majesty and dignity;
>   clothe yourself with glory and splendor.
> Pour out the overflowings of your anger,
>   and look on everyone who is proud and abase him.
> Look on everyone who is proud and bring him low
>   and tread down the wicked where they stand.
> Hide them all in the dust together;
>   bind their faces in the world below.
> Then will I also acknowledge to you
>   that your own right hand can save you. (40:9–14)

God alone can abase the proud. He alone is Lord over history. Job lacked God's power, as well as his majesty, dignity, glory, and splendor. Consequently, he couldn't force God to vindicate him. If justice was to be done and Job was to be vindicated, then God would have to do it.

God's speeches reiterated that he is both Creator and Lord. Consequently, his perspective is vastly different from ours, at once perfectly detailed and comprehensively panoramic. As the world's maker and sustainer, he alone knows the story of the world's beginning, middle, and end. In other words, he alone fully knows and completely rules over the natural and moral worlds.[21]

At the end of God's speeches, Job finally understood:

> I know that you can do all things;
>   no purpose of yours can be thwarted. . . .
> Surely I spoke of things I did not understand,
>   things too wonderful for me to know. . . .

My ears had heard of you
>   but now my eyes have seen you.
Therefore I despise myself
>   and repent in dust and ashes. (42:2–3, 5–6 NIV)

Job had driven himself to despair by insisting on getting an explanation for his suffering and then settling too quickly on what seemed
to be the best explanation. He thought he could make sense of what
was happening to him only by concluding that God was being unfair.
Hadn't he always shown *chesed* to everyone around him? And wasn't he
right, then, to expect *chesed* from them? Shouldn't he have hoped his
righteousness would ultimately be rewarded?[h]

Yes, his hope was warranted, but he had been expecting his rewards
too soon. God sovereignly delayed them for reasons Job could not even
guess at.

Job's despair drives home how hard it can be for even the godliest
among us to keep perspective and thus avoid acquiring false beliefs in the
midst of great suffering. Yet his despair was unwarranted. Job thought he
knew the end of his story—that his eye would never again see good—when
only the world's maker and sustainer knows such things. Yet Job's final
chapter shows him comfortably at home again. Moreover, even though he
had hastily declared that God had wronged him, God in his steadfast love
considered Job's words as a whole to have been right (see 42:7). So God in
his *chesed* may consider us faithful in the midst of profound suffering even
when in our perplexity we actively question what he is doing. Indeed, he
may even forgive our settling, like Job, on a false explanation.[22]

Scenes of a Faithful, Hopeful, and Bold Jeremiah
Jeremiah's words in Jeremiah 20:7 seem to imply that he was even more
deeply disoriented by the events climaxing in his clash with Pashhur
than Job was by the aggravations accompanying his prolonged illness.
Job usually believed that if he could confront God, then God would

---

h. For evidence that Job practiced *chesed*, see 29:11–17. For his expectations stemming from
that, see 29:18–20 and especially 31:3: "Is not calamity for the unrighteous, and disaster for the
workers of iniquity?"

be fair to him. But it seems Jeremiah was not merely tempted to doubt God's fairness to him. He also came to think that God had deceived him.[23] In fact, his words may suggest that he was tempted to believe God was not good, period. Job's suffering tempted him to adopt false beliefs about his future and God's posture toward him, but Jeremiah's ordeal prompted him to believe falsehoods about God.

Nothing in his book shows Jeremiah deliberately reorienting himself after his crisis in chapter 20. Yet the words that follow his despairing cry at the very end of that chapter—"Why did I come out from the womb to see toil and sorrow, and spend my days in shame?"—are simply these: "This is the word that came to Jeremiah from the LORD" (Jer. 21:1).

This new word did not come to him immediately. His accusations and curses in chapter 20 probably took place sometime between 609–605 BC, while the events recorded at the beginning of chapter 21 probably took place around 588 BC—or, in other words, about twenty years later. From chapter 21 onward, much of the book is nonchronological, with its seemingly haphazard structure probably reflecting and indeed confirming the trauma that almost continuously accompanied Jeremiah's life. As Paul House observes, the book "may be shaped as it is because Baruch and Jeremiah wrote it piecemeal in the midst of their turbulent lives," with the result being that it "reads more like what political prisoners and refugees write than what persons writing in settled places and times produce."[24] People who are suffering or have suffered in particularly awful ways don't tend to write coherent narratives.

Yet whenever the new word of chapter 21 came, Jeremiah proclaimed it boldly. His desire to renounce his prophetic office had vanished, even though he was imprisoned for proclaiming this new word (see Jer. 32–38). He no longer despaired.[25] In fact, even though he knew that the inhabitants of Judah and Jerusalem were about to go into exile, he bought a field from a kinsman in order to show that he believed God's word that God's people would someday return and again buy houses, fields, and vineyards in the promised land (see 32:1–25), and he confidently proclaimed the Lord's plans for a bright hope and a future for the exiles (see 29:4, 10–14).

Virtually all of what is found in Jeremiah 21–45 can be assigned dates in the last twenty years of Jeremiah's ministry, after his mistreatment at the hand of Pashhur the priest as reported in chapter 20. Chapters 21, 29, and 32 portray him as having recovered his faith, hope, and strength. What accounted for this? We aren't told. Yet the same Jeremiah who reacted so negatively to the events recorded in chapter 20 began performing his prophetic tasks again.

The books of Ruth and Job present us with complete stories, stories that progress from their beginnings through their middles to their ends. Naomi's and Job's lives come full circle. Both stories end happily. So they teach us that a suffering saint's pessimistic predictions about how his or her earthly story will end are uncertain at best. They also show that the quality of a suffering saint's future is not entirely dependent on whether he or she can faithfully muster up true beliefs. In fact, a suffering saint's future doesn't even depend on whether he or she can avoid believing a false story. In spite of Naomi's believing otherwise, it was in the end still fitting to call her "Pleasant," and Job received again a fitting earthly reward for his righteousness when the Lord blessed his "latter days . . . more than his beginning." His eye again saw good.[26]

Jeremiah's story is incomplete. Near the end of his book we read, "Thus far are the words of Jeremiah" (Jer. 51:64). Nothing more is said about him. We are not even told that he died. His book just breaks off. And his story does not end happily. Yet from chapter 21 onward we see that Jeremiah regained his hope and faithfully fulfilled his prophetic office in spite of his ongoing suffering. His story teaches us that a saint's future does not depend on whether he can always avoid protesting against his story or restrain himself from uttering what are blasphemies or near blasphemies. Of course, God's people must do all they can to avoid such failings. Yet the quality of Jeremiah's future ultimately hinged on nothing other than the reality of God's steadfast love for him. Because of his *chesed* for Jeremiah, "the God who gives endurance and encouragement" (Rom. 15:5 NIV) restored Jeremiah's hope, even though he never gave him earthly peace, security, or happiness.

We don't know if Lamentations was written by Jeremiah. Yet its author's experience as reported in its third chapter mirrors the sea change in Jeremiah's experience that transpired between chapters 1–20 and 21–52. Lamentations' anonymous author began by declaring:

> I am the man who has seen affliction
>> under the rod of [God's] wrath;
> he has driven and brought me
>> into darkness without any light. . . .
>
> He has besieged and enveloped me
>> with bitterness and tribulation. . . .
>
> My soul is bereft of peace;
>> I have forgotten what happiness is;
> so I say, "My endurance has perished;
>> so has my hope from the Lord." (Lam. 3:1–2, 5, 17–18)

In terms of his own resources and from his own perspective, this man was at the end of his tether. All of life's stars had disappeared, and so despair—which comes from a Latin word meaning *the complete loss of hope*—had conquered him. "But this," he then reported, "I call to mind, *and therefore I have hope: . . . The Lord will not cast off forever, but, though he cause grief, he will have compassion according to the abundance of his steadfast love*; for he does not [willingly] afflict . . . or grieve the children of men" (Lam. 3:21, 31–33).

Jeremiah made a similar appeal to God's *chesed* as the ground for his exiled people's hope in his book's thirty-third chapter:

> Thus says the Lord: In this place of which you say, "It is a waste without man or beast," in the cities of Judah and the streets of Jerusalem that are desolate, without man or inhabitant or beast, there shall be heard again the voice of mirth and the voice of gladness, the voice of the bridegroom and the voice of the bride, the voices of those who sing, as they bring thank offerings to the house of the Lord:

> "Give thanks to the LORD of hosts,
>   for the LORD is good,
>   for his steadfast love endures forever!" (Jer. 33:10–11)

Biblical faith and hope are grounded in God's self-revelation that— no matter how dark and hopeless life may now seem—his saints will ultimately know him as "the God of *chesed*," for that is indeed his name. As the final verse of Psalm 23 affirms: "Surely your goodness and unfailing love [*chesed*] will pursue me all the days of my life, *and I will live in the house of the LORD forever*" (NLT).

Some Final Thoughts

And so we can conclude from the stories of these Old Testament saints that the true Christian story is both sobering and encouraging. We, like they, may face seasons of sorrow and suffering so profound that our faith and hope waver and perhaps even seem to die. We may find ourselves protesting against the story we are in and even be tempted to rebel against it. Yet God in his steadfast love will continue to pursue us, as Paul's repetition of this "trustworthy" saying in 2 Timothy 2, implies:

> If we have died with [Christ], we will also live with him;
> if we endure, we will also reign with him;
> if we deny him, he also will deny us;
> if we are faithless, he remains faithful—
> *for he cannot deny himself.* (2:11–13; cf. Matt. 10:33)

The God who characterizes himself as abounding in *chesed*—the God who in the New Testament reveals himself as the Father of our Lord Jesus Christ—cannot deny himself, and so even when our suffering prompts us to lose so much perspective that our faith and hope flicker and seem to die, he will remain faithful as long as we don't explicitly, decisively, and permanently deny him. To lose faith and hope is nothing like forevermore repudiating the only one who can save us (see Heb. 6:4–8 and 10:28–31 with Acts 4:12 and Rom. 10:9–13).[i] Naomi, Job, and

---

i. Peter impulsively denied his Lord but repented afterward (Matt. 26:30–35, 69–75).

Jeremiah didn't deny their Lord, so all their errors, protests, and failings were forgiven them.

MAINTAINING PERSPECTIVE

The New Testament does warn us, however, against losing our faith and hope. It declares that they need to remain strong and unwavering, because God is not pleased with those who shrink back (see Heb. 10:38). Once we have become convinced of the truth of the Christian story, embraced it, and begun living its storyline—once we have, using our Lord's words, put our hands to the plow—we must not let anything, not even our suffering, interrupt our continuing to live it.

Ultimately, our staying faithful and hopeful in the midst of profound suffering does not depend entirely on us. Yet there are steps we can take to maintain our perspective. First, we must remember that *chesed*—steadfast, kind, loyal, and merciful loving concern for others—is basic to God's character and emblematic of all he is. Second, we must appeal to God's *chesed* whenever we need reassurance of his radical and unceasing care for us. Third, we must believe that God is able to do all that his *chesed* intends for us. Suffering, we must remind ourselves, may pursue us in this lifetime, but God's invincible power guarantees that the joy implicit in our being the recipients of God's *chesed* will come to us with the morning.[j] And, last, we must "read, mark, learn, and inwardly digest"[27] biblical stories like Naomi's, Job's, and Jeremiah's that trace God's steadfast and unstoppable love for his saints through the starless darkness of their profound suffering. The truths that held for them will hold for us, and so we must apply them to every one of our personal stories.

Sometimes we can do no more than merely endure. And as Jeremiah's story shows, suffering can test our ability to do even that. It may be all we can do simply to avoid denying our Lord. As the clouds of suffering rolled over Naomi, Job, and Jeremiah, they lost their bearings. Things appeared so dark it seemed nothing good could lie ahead. So their hopes vanished. They even began taking false bearings that led

---

j. "Weeping may last through the night, but joy comes with the morning" (Ps. 30:5 NLT).

them to believe falsehoods—most crucially, the falsehood that God was no longer manifesting his steadfast love to them.

We now know they were wrong. Their stories teach us that appearance is not always reality. What appears at some point to be the story of a life may not be what the full story of that life actually and finally is. God was still working for their good.

This can help us to hope even in horrific circumstances. By all means, let us strive to maintain our faith and hope by practicing the psalmists' breathing lessons and focusing on stories like Naomi's, Job's, and Jeremiah's that show that things are not always as they seem. Naomi's story shows that God may be working far beyond whatever we can ask or even imagine. And Job's story shows that if God's saints were always to know what he was doing, then that would sometimes defeat God's purposes.

And so even God's apparent indifference to Graham's suffering does not imply that God abandoned him. I have no reason to believe Graham denied his Lord. Nor do I know what God may have been teaching him. Could Graham have learned something through the calamity of his life's end that will shine throughout eternity? If we have grasped the depths of Naomi's, Job's, and Jeremiah's suffering, then who are we to say that God must not ever work good for his saints in fearsome ways?[28]

Right now, Graham's parents are suffering profoundly. They have been tempted at times to rebel against their story, to deny and repudiate their Lord and his ways. But the end of their son's story may be resplendent with glories neither they nor we can now see. Certainly we should pray that at the consummation they will lift their tearful, now sometimes defiant eyes and say, "Oh, now we see!"

In my future volumes we must still address many issues and seek answers to many questions. But keeping these Old Testament lessons in mind can help us breathe, endure, and keep our faith. Indeed, as Paul wrote, "everything that was written in former times was written for our instruction, *so that through endurance and through encouragement of the scriptures we may have hope*" (Rom. 15:4 NET).

EPILOGUE

Living within the Full Christian Story

Therefore, since we are surrounded
by so great a cloud of witnesses,
let us also lay aside every weight, and sin which clings so closely,
and let us run with endurance the race that is set before us,
looking to Jesus, the founder and perfecter of our faith,
who for the joy that was set before him endured the cross,
despising the shame,
and is seated at the right hand of the throne of God.

Hebrews 12:1–2

The creation waits with eager longing
for the revealing of the sons of God.
For the creation was subjected to futility . . .
in hope that the creation itself will be set free
from its bondage to corruption and obtain the
freedom of the glory of the children of God. . . .
And not only the creation,
but we ourselves . . . groan inwardly
as we wait eagerly for adoption as sons, the redemption of our bodies.
For in this hope we were saved.

Romans 8:19–21, 23–24

We rejoice in our sufferings,
knowing that suffering produces endurance,

and endurance produces character,
and character produces hope, and hope does not put us to shame,
because God's love has been poured into our hearts
through the Holy Spirit who has been given to us.

Romans 5:3–5

The Spirit himself bears witness with our spirit
that we are children of God,
and if children, then heirs—heirs of God
and fellow heirs with Christ,
provided we suffer with him
in order that we may also be glorified with him.

Romans 8:16–17

This volume has focused on some of God's Old Testament saints whose suffering is recounted at greater length and in much more detail than even our Lord's suffering in the New Testament.[1] As we shall see especially in my fourth volume, we Christians must understand our suffering within the context of our Lord's suffering, yet Old Testament stories like Naomi's, Job's, and Jeremiah's exhibit how difficult the lives of God's people may be. Their individual circumstances differed, yet each suffered profoundly. They each experienced something so deep and disruptive that it dominated their consciousness and threatened to overwhelm them, tempting them to lose hope that their lives could ever be good again.[a] Yet God had not abandoned them. Consequently, if we suffer profoundly, it does not mean that God has abandoned us. Indeed, the God of *chesed* is always present in the midst of his saints' suffering, accomplishing his good purposes for them in and through it, no matter how incomprehensible at the time it may be.

---

a. See chap. 1, p. 14.

SUMMING UP

"Here on earth," our Lord told his disciples, "you will have many trials and sorrows" (John 16:33 NLT). "All who desire to live a godly life in Christ Jesus," Paul reminded Timothy, "will be persecuted" (2 Tim. 3:12). Yet, our Lord reiterated, we must endure to the end to be saved (see Matt. 10:22; 24:13; cf. Luke 21:19). His call for endurance reverberates throughout the New Testament (see, e.g., 2 Cor. 1:6; 1 Pet. 2:19–20; Rev. 14:9–12).[2] That call is strongest in the book of Hebrews, which was written to urge its recipients to keep their faith and hope alive.

Hebrews' author describes his book as a brief "word of exhortation" (Heb. 13:22),[3] which he prepared for a very small local congregation of Jewish Christians who had remained faithful and hopeful in spite of strong persecution. Some of them had been publicly mistreated. Some had been imprisoned. Some had had their property confiscated, which they nevertheless "joyfully accepted . . . because [they] knew [they] had better and lasting possessions" (10:33–34 NIV). But in the face of new persecution, some were tempted to abandon their faith. This threat prompted Hebrews' anonymous author to warn them of the eternal consequences of denying their Lord as well as to show what remaining faithful and hopeful would bring.

We Must Strive to Keep Our Faith and Hope Alive

As we saw near the end of chapter 4, profound suffering may assail our faith and hope so severely that they waver and almost die, yet the God who abounds in *chesed* will remain faithful to us as long as we don't decisively deny him.[4] Our faith and hope need to remain strong and steady, for we must walk by faith and not by sight (see 2 Cor. 5:6–10; Col. 1:21–23; Heb. 3:6, 14), and God takes no pleasure in those who shrink back (see Heb. 3:6; 10:38).

Hebrews 11 shows why we must strive to keep our faith and hope alive. It opens by declaring that "faith shows the reality of what we hope for; it is the evidence of things we cannot see" (1:1 NLT).[5] In other words, faith reveals what will actually come to be, which we then hope for. By faith, God's Old Testament saints attested to realities that were by their very nature unseeable or yet unseen.[6]

By the faith of his Old Testament saints, God brought into being the earlier stages of his redemptive plan. For instance, by faith Abraham obeyed when God told him to leave his homeland and head for a place he would receive as an inheritance, even though, as he stepped out, he didn't know where he was going (see Heb. 11:8). "By faith," we are told, "he went to live in the land of promise" (11:9; cf. Gen. 12:1–4 with Gal. 3:16). Consequently, "from one man, and him as good as dead, were born descendants as many as the stars of heaven and as many as the innumerable grains of sand by the seashore" (11:12)[7]—descendants including God's own Son (see Matt. 1:1–2; Luke 3:23–34).

Again, it was by faith that Moses, even though he had grown up as the son of Pharaoh's daughter, refused to be called her son, choosing "to share the oppression of God's people instead of enjoying the fleeting pleasures of sin" (11:25 NLT). By faith he left Egypt, being unafraid of Pharaoh's anger, and "kept right on going" until he reached the Midianite wilderness "because he kept his eyes on the one who is invisible" (11:27 NLT).[8] Later, the same faith, which believes that God exists and rewards those who earnestly seek him (see 11:6), led him to institute the first Passover so that when the Lord's destroyer passed through Egypt killing all of Egypt's firstborn, he was not permitted to touch any of the Israelites (see 11:28 with Ex. 12:21–28).

Hebrews' author claims that time would have failed him if he had tried to recount all the individuals "who through faith conquered kingdoms, enforced justice, obtained promises, stopped the mouths of lions, quenched the power of fire, escaped the edge of the sword, were made strong out of weakness, became mighty in war, put foreign armies to flight" and even "received back their dead by resurrection" (11:33–35). Yet the faith of others meant that some "were tortured, refusing to accept release, so that they might rise again to a better life" and others "suffered mocking and flogging, and even chains and imprisonment." Some "were stoned, . . . sawn in two, . . . killed with the sword," and yet others "went about in skins of sheep and goats, destitute, afflicted, mistreated—of whom the world was not worthy—wandering about in deserts and mountains, and in dens and caves of the earth" (11:35-38).

The unseen future realities that were to become the earlier stages of God's redemptive plan came into being as God's Old Testament saints lived out their faith. In other words, God ordained their faith and obedience as essential steps in the realization of his redemptive plan that would culminate in the earthly work of his Son, Jesus Christ. God often works through his saints' work (see, e.g., Phil. 2:12-13). This amounts to saying that if Abraham had not stepped out in obedience to his Lord's command to head for an unknown place, then there would have been no Isaac, no Jacob, and no Old Testament people of God through whom all the nations of the earth would be blessed (see Gen. 22:18). If Moses had not believed what he had heard about God's promise to deliver Abraham's enslaved descendants from foreign oppression (see Gen. 15:13-14), then he would not have obeyed God's call to deliver them from Egyptian slavery and lead them to the Promised Land (see Ex. 6:2-8)—and then there never would have been a nation of Israel, "distinct . . . from every other people on the face of the earth" (Ex. 33:16).[9]

As we saw in chapter 1, stories orient us by placing us somewhere on a trajectory that has a beginning, middle, and end.[b] I must believe a personal story that orients me to the particular people, places, and things around me, describing where I have come from, where I am right now, and where I think I can go so that I can then project myself into a hopeful future. I also need to believe some big, general story that orients me regarding what human life means. From the first glimmer of the good news that our Lord Jesus Christ would defeat the devil's work by dying on a cross in Genesis 3:15,[c] God has been gradually and progressively revealing the general story about what our lives actually mean. By faith, the saints in Hebrews 11 believed God and thus oriented themselves by whatever portion of the storyline he had revealed to them. By obediently living out their faith in that portion of the story, they kept in motion the series of events that culminated in the appearance of our Lord.

---

b. See chap. 1, pp. 20-21; also chap. 4, pp. 63-65.
c. This is known as the *protevangelium*. Much more on it in my second volume.

And so they were "doers of [God's] word, and not hearers only" (James 1:22). In Scripture, *hearing* God involves not only *listening* to him and *believing* what he says but also *obeying* him—*doing* what he says.[10]

By hearing and obeying God's word, the Old Testament saints mentioned in Hebrews 11 made real the substance of God's promises.[d] *Their* faith, hope, and obedience opened the way for the incarnation of our Lord and thus were God's instrument for securing *our* salvation. Our living faith and hope are born of their faith, hope, and obedience, for they were the means by which God was preparing for our redemption in Christ.[11] Without their faith, hope, and obedience, we Christians would not be.[12] So we, too, must strive to keep our faith and hope alive. In everyday life as well as in the Scriptures, it is not merely believing but doing that makes real the substance of our hopes. We must strive to be faithful, hopeful, and obedient for the sake of those who will come after us. As Hebrews' author urged his hearers, "let us consider how to stir up one another to love and good works, . . . encouraging one another, and all the more as you see the Day drawing near" (10:24–25). One way we do this is by imitating "those who through faith and patience inherit the promises" (Heb. 6:12).

What Does It Mean to Be Faithful and Hopeful?

Right in the middle of his account of Moses's faith in Hebrews 11, Hebrews' author made a puzzling claim. After having observed that Moses "chose to share the oppression of God's people instead of enjoying the fleeting pleasures of sin" (11:25 NLT), he wrote that Moses "thought it was better to suffer for the sake of Christ than to own the treasures of Egypt, for he was looking ahead to his great reward" (11:26 NLT). It is because he thought "it was better to suffer for the sake of Christ" that Moses by faith "left the land of Egypt, not fearing the king's anger" and "kept right on going" until he arrived in the Midian wilderness (11:27

---

d. As suggested by the Authorized Version's translation of Heb. 11:1, "Now faith is the *substance* of things hoped for, the evidence of things not seen." The actions of the Old Testament saints arising out of their faith *brought into being*—in other words, *made substantial*—realities that were essential steps along the way to the still future and final realization of God's promises at the consummation.

NLT with Ex. 2:15). This claim that Moses "thought it was better to suffer *for the sake of Christ* than to own the treasures of Egypt" should puzzle us. Does it mean that Moses knew that God's redemptive plan would culminate in the work of his Son, Jesus Christ? No. Yet it also does not mean that Hebrews' author was stretching the truth. There is a very deep truth here about what it means to embrace a story that places us somewhere on a trajectory aimed at achieving a particular end.

Think about the high schooler I mentioned in chapter 4. She decided to embrace the storyline that is meant to end in her becoming a primary-care physician. She will achieve that goal only if she believes she can become a doctor and then acts in ways that move her along the pathway that will end with her becoming a PCP. She must take the intermediate steps—finishing high school and college, maintaining high grades, applying to medical schools and so on—in order for her hope to become a doctor to be realized.

As she does so, she is already participating in the reality of becoming a PCP. The full reality is not yet hers, but she is already participating in the reality of, for instance, learning some of the science that will enable her to make well-grounded medical judgments. She does not yet know the full reality of actually being a PCP. Indeed, she can only dimly imagine that reality now, and the actual reality will differ significantly from what she imagines it will be, just as the reality of married life differs from what engaged couples imagine it will be. Yet by embracing the storyline that is meant to result in her becoming a PCP, she has already embarked on the trajectory that will end in her being one—and to whatever degree she has embarked on that trajectory, she is already beginning to live the story that will culminate in her being a PCP. Her current suffering—for working hard at her studies rather than playing is a kind of mild suffering, in the sense of being something that she probably sometimes wishes didn't have to be—is then properly seen as suffering for the sake of becoming a PCP.

Similarly, when Moses "chose to share the oppression of God's people instead of enjoying the fleeting pleasures of sin," he did not know that God's redemptive plan would culminate in the work of his

Son, Jesus Christ. Yet his sharing in their suffering was "for the sake of Christ" because it embraced the same kind of disgrace and alienation our Lord suffered when he, as Hebrews' author put it, "suffered outside the city gate to make the people holy through his own blood" (Heb. 13:12 NLT).[13] Moses suffered *outside Egypt's gates* by departing for Midian rather than owning the treasures of Egypt. He understood that his suffering was somehow part of God's redemptive story and thus embraced the trajectory that would culminate in our Lord's work.[14] In that way, he indeed suffered for our Lord's sake, for his suffering was an intrinsic part of God's unfolding story.

Because God's revelation of the full Christian story has been gradual and progressive, his saints' faithfulness and hopefulness have always involved their embracing its trajectory *whether they explicitly knew what the story was all about or not.* And by believing and obeying God's will to the degree that he has revealed it, we also participate in that reality.

Knowing God's Redemptive Plan

If our high schooler's life has purpose and meaning because she has embraced the storyline that is meant to result in her becoming a PCP, then she needs to thank someone. For she didn't cook up that story by herself. Someone told her about medicine, doctors, and primary-care physicians. In fact, none of us cook up our own stories. Other people orient us by telling us where we have come from, where we are, and where we can go. In general, we become aware of life's various storylines only by being told about them, and we embrace some particular storyline only after hearing about it in some way. My college mentors pitched the possibility of my becoming a philosophy professor and then encouraged me to embark on the course of study that made that possibility a reality.

Likewise, we cannot embrace the Christian storyline unless we are told about it (see Rom. 10:14–17), for it involves "a secret and hidden wisdom of God" that no one can know unless God reveals it (1 Cor. 2:7). And so our confidence in its truth depends on our believing that God has revealed it to us—that he has told us his thoughts and plans regarding what will be. It is only because God's Spirit "searches . . . even the depths of God" (v. 10) and then has told us what "God has prepared for those who love him" that we are able to understand "what God has freely given us," what he has "destined for our glory before time began" (see vv. 9, 12, 7 NIV). God's plans for his people, as we shall see in my third volume, have always been settled and in place. They cannot be stymied. And so we, as God's people, by having received his Spirit (see v. 12), are enabled to attest to future realities that are yet unseen, and then to live out our faith in ways that help to bring the later stages of God's redemptive plan to life.

As we shall see in my second volume, God has been revealing his plans for us from the time he created Adam and Eve. The progressive revelation of his plans—of "the true story of the whole world"[15]—is enshrined in Scripture. We know this storyline by his telling us about it as we listen to him speak to us by his Spirit through the words of Scripture.

We cannot understand what human life really means without hearing this story, and so *hearing* is our most important sense.[16] It was by hearing and obeying God that Abram—which means "exalted father"— became Abraham—the "father of a multitude of nations" (Gen. 17:5)— through whom all the nations of the earth would be blessed (see Gen. 12:4; 26:4; Gal. 3:8). By understanding that God would reward him for his obedience, Moses could think it "better to suffer for the sake of Christ than to own the treasures of Egypt, *for he was looking ahead to his great reward*" (Heb. 11:26 NLT).

Faith, Hope, and Suffering in the Book of Hebrews

As they faced the prospect of renewed suffering, Hebrews' author reminded his hearers that they needed endurance to do God's will and thus receive his promises (see 10:36). That led him to recount what God's Old Testament saints did by faith in chapter 11 and then to remind them of our Lord's endurance at the beginning of chapter 12. Hebrews 11 teaches that while God's Old Testament saints accomplished much by faith, none received what was promised (see 11:13, 39). They only saw and greeted the realities faith revealed "from afar" and thus "acknowledged that they were strangers and exiles on the earth" (11:13).

By having "died in faith" (11:13)—that is, still hoping and indeed yearning for what they had not yet received—they attest to us, "*the Christian community* of the reality of a heavenly homeland"[17] and show us what our attitude must be as we seek the same realities (see 11:4, 14; 12:1). The principle of faith as trust in God's eschatological promises knows that those promises will never find their true fulfillment in this world.[e] We know by faith that God has prepared a future homeland for his saints, which will be "the city of the living God, the heavenly Jerusalem" (Heb. 12:22) that will descend from heaven at the consummation. It will bring us into God's everlasting presence and deliver us from all suffering (see Rev. 21:1-4, 9-14; 22:14). Because his Old Testament saints desired this city and thus showed themselves to have embraced their Lord's redemptive storyline, he was not ashamed to be called their God (see Heb. 11:16).[18]

Hebrews 11 shows that acknowledging that the story is unfinished is essential to biblical faith.[19] Hoping for what is not yet is, then, essential to embracing the biblical storyline. Having faith and having hope are two sides of the same coin: "*faith* shows the reality of what we *hope* for; *it is the evidence of things we cannot see*" (Heb. 11:1 NLT). It is *by* faith and *in* hope that we are saved as we wait "with anticipation and assurance for the culmination of God's plan for us and the world."[20] Both faith and hope focus on what is yet unseen. Until our Lord returns, all of God's saints must live by faith and hope *and not by sight.*

Hebrews 11 also shows that the life of faith may involve prolonged suffering. It notes, for instance, that Abraham, Isaac, and Jacob never possessed the land that God promised Abraham would someday belong to his descendants (11:9, 13)—"not even a foot's length" of it (Acts 7:5). All three remained strangers and foreigners who lacked all native and civil rights. They always lived in tents (see Heb. 11:9), signifying "that believers are pilgrims and strangers whose goal is yet before them."[21] Saintly life in this world is necessarily nomadic, "for here we have no lasting city, but we seek the city that is to come" (Heb. 13:14).

---

e. Since eschatology involves history's final events (see chap. 4, n. f), God's *eschatological promises* will be fulfilled only at the Christian storyline's consummation.

Faith, Hope, and Suffering in the Rest of Scripture

The life of faith may also involve all sorts of profound suffering. Genesis records much suffering in the lives of Abraham's descendants. Isaac and Rebekah endured forty years of childlessness, while always being acutely aware that God's promise to Abraham that his descendants would be as numerous as the stars would be fulfilled only through them. Their son Jacob was a locus of double dealing and family strife. Other Old Testament passages show God's saints undergoing lifelong illness (see Psalm 88), deformity,[f] and imprisonment (see, e.g., Gen. 39:20; Jer. 37:11–15). In the New Testament we read in addition of martyrdom (see Acts 7:54–8:3; Rev. 2:12–13), loneliness (see 2 Tim. 1:15; 4:9–11), sickness (see Gal. 4:13; 2 Tim. 4:20), chronic weakness (see 1 Tim. 5:23), and helplessness in old age (see John 21:18). And so it is natural for us to ask, Are there any limits to how we as God's people may suffer?

Romans 8 observes that God has subjected his creation to futility, corruption, and decay because of Adam and Eve's sin (see Rom. 8:20–21 with Gen. 3:14–19). This means "not only that the universe is running down (as we would say), but that nature is also enslaved, locked into an unending cycle, so that conception, birth and growth are relentlessly followed by decline, decay, death and decomposition."[22] Verse 22 then mentions pain. In sum, John Stott writes, "creation is out of joint because [it is] under judgment." And since we as God's saints are part of creation, even we are subject to virtually all of the physical, psychological, and moral frailties and defects that can befall humankind.

This includes not only life's ordinary afflictions—such as getting a cold, being weary at the end of a long day's work, or breaking a leg—but also the possibility of our experiencing moral horrors, such as a brother killing a brother (see Gen. 4:1–16) or a stepbrother raping his sister and then the sister's full brother taking revenge (see 2 Sam. 13:1–33). We may know wrenching poverty (see Luke 21:1–4) or orphanhood (see Lam. 5:1–6). We may suffer treachery at the hands of close friends (see Pss. 41; 55) or face war, slavery, and perhaps even starvation (see Lam.

---

f. Lev. 21:16–24 prohibits the blind, lame, or physically defective from serving as Old Testament priests, which means such deformities occurred among God's people.

2:11–12). Most of us will experience the depredations of old age (see 2 Sam. 19:31–35; 1 Kings 1:1–4), with some of us getting Alzheimer's. A few of us may also experience repulsive and disfiguring diseases (see Job and Ps. 88). We may have to cope with lifelong singleness or same-sex orientation.[23] We may lose loved ones to mass murder[g] or tragic accidents. We may be confronted with mental illness (see Pss. 42; 43)[24] or suicide (see 2 Sam. 17:23). In short, there is virtually nothing that any human being can suffer that may not befall God's children or his children's children.[25]

Yet acknowledging these possibilities, Paul declared, should prompt us to hope earnestly for the consummation rather than cause us to despair, because we know, by faith, that none of our suffering, no matter how difficult or horrific it may be, is "worth comparing with the glory that will be revealed in us."[26] The creation, Paul wrote, waits in eager expectation for us—the children of God—to be revealed (see Rom. 8:18–19). And then creation itself "will be set free from its bondage to corruption and obtain the freedom of the glory of the children of God" (v. 21).[27]

Believing that this is what God has in store for us is essential to Christian faith. We can be confident of it because the Holy Spirit indwells us and attests to its truth. Indeed, we must understand any anguish we experience now as labor pains that herald our full future adoption as God's children, including the redemption of our bodies (see Rom. 8:23 and John 16:16–22). It is by this hope that we are saved. This is the storyline we have begun living by faith. And an essential aspect of our living this story is our recognizing that "hope that is seen is not hope. For who hopes for what he sees? But if we hope for what we do not see, we wait for it with patience" (Rom. 8:24–25).

Ultimately, our waiting with patience requires keeping our more distant goals in mind. Our high schooler can survive a bad midterm test score in a difficult class by remembering that her score at the end of the term is more important—and that even that final score is only

---

g. See chap. 2, endnote 1.

important in the larger scheme of her being admitted to a good college where she can prepare for medical school. At each step along her pathway she needs to be thinking in terms of the next steps that she must take in order to realize her hope of becoming a PCP. As she takes each step, her grasp of later steps and of her final goal is being refined. When she begins attending rounds as a medical student, some of the realities of practicing medicine will finally become clear to her. By the time she starts to practice as a PCP, she will know that what she had initially imagined about being a doctor was incomplete, inaccurate, and fanciful in many ways.

Likewise regarding Christian hope. By noting that the patriarchs all died in faith, not having received what God had promised, Hebrews shows that by postponing his fulfillment of his promise to give them the land, God enabled them to see that theirs was not to be an earthly reward. By the end of his life, Abraham knew he could only look up and forward to a heavenly home. At the end of their earthly lives, he and Isaac and Jacob knew by the eyes of faith that God had never destined them to be anything but strangers and exiles. Each was then positioned to understand—that is, to know by faith—that "here we have no lasting city, but we seek the city that is to come" (Heb. 13:14). And because they acknowledged that that was what God had prepared for them, he was not ashamed to be called their God.

God's apparent delay in fulfilling his promises refines our hopes. We lift our heads and see God's eschatological rewards from afar as our earthly hopes die.[28] Our suffering inclines us to reorient our hopes toward the consummation. We are sinful, silly, distractible creatures who inevitably major on what is minor if suffering doesn't stop us. Our suffering often needs to be long and hard in order for us to learn the lessons God is teaching. It can be very difficult for us to maintain our faith and hope in the midst of his lessons. Like the Old Testament saints we have studied, our faith may waver and our hope dim. But then we must remind ourselves that our suffering is part of God's refining fire. God uses it to strengthen and purify our faith and hope. And what he has begun, he will complete.

In the meantime, when we suffer as we now know we must, we brace ourselves in the conflict between the *already* of Christian suffering and the *not yet* of Christian glory. We remind ourselves of how God has rescued his saints in the past. We lament as a way of casting all our cares on him because we know he cares for us. We strive to persevere because we know that God is not pleased with those who shrink back. And above all we keep the example of our Lord and his unparalleled suffering for our sake before us (Heb. 12:1–3).

Yet the ground of our hope is deeper still. It is rooted in our overwhelming sense of the steadfast love—the *chesed*—of God, who while we were yet sinners sent his Son, Jesus Christ, to die for us. God's love in sending his Son is brought home to our hearts by the Spirit who indwells us. It floods our hearts and anchors our emotional lives.

When profound suffering strikes, it can seem that all of the stars that have guided our Christian lives have disappeared. And yet the core of Christian faith is the belief that God sovereignly controls all of life's storms and that he can—*and indeed ultimately will*—see his people safely through even the worst storms. We have his word and the experience of his saints in Scripture that when those storms finally begin to subside and the sky begins to clear, we will look up and once again see the sun and the moon and the stars, and then realize that our loving heavenly Father has indeed been with us all along our way. This may not happen in this lifetime, but then it *will* happen in the one to come.

ACKNOWLEDGMENTS

When the Lord revealed his glory to Moses, the only characteristic of his name that he proclaimed twice was his *chesed*—his *steadfast* (or *unfailing*) *love, kindness,* and *faithfulness.* The LORD's *chesed,* David declared at the end of Psalm 23, is always unremittingly pursuing his saints: "Surely your goodness and unfailing love will pursue me all the days of my life, and I will live in the house of the LORD forever" (v. 6 NLT).

Our God often channels his *chesed* through his saints' *chesed,* where it is seen in the sort of love of God and neighbor that moves one person to act unselfishly for another's benefit.

This and the subsequent volumes in this series would never have been written if it weren't for the *chesed* that others have shown me.

When I went to college a little over a year after I suffered a paralyzing accident, three men in particular showed me steadfast love, kindness, and faithfulness: David McKenna, the new president of (then) Seattle Pacific College; Frank Kline, the dean of religion; and Cliff McCrath, the dean of students. They gave me literally hundreds of hours of their friendship, affection, and counsel—and I would be unrecognizable today if it weren't for the ways that their unfailing love seeded everything that I have since become.

Three people, one during my college years and two during my work on this volume, have by their careful reading set the tone for my writing: Donald McNichols, one of my college English professors; Tess Fawell; and Nancy Duperreault.

In more recent years, the unfailing support and encouragement of three more persons has been crucial to my work: Tory Houriet, Paul Winters, and Buck McCabe. Christian Scholars' Fund has generously supported my work by helping to relieve my course load at Wheaton College over the past eight years so that I would have more time to think and write.

The gestation of this volume has been lengthy—over ten years. During that time, many of my students have read earlier drafts of what is now before you, testing them for coherence and clarity. Among the most helpful and encouraging have been Sophie Bouwsma, Michaela Bylsma, Josh Fort, Cameron Harro, Isaiah Jeong, Ben Meyer, Adriana Moore, Gareth Phillips, Michael Rau, Karis (Edwards) Riley, Kirsten Ryken Collins, Micah Stucki, and Marshall Thompson. Students in my PHIL 241: Suffering courses at the college have asked important questions and added worthwhile insights.

Crossway has been very patient as I worked out the details of what was once projected as a single, fairly short volume. Justin Taylor and Lane Dennis deserve special mention.

Portions of this volume have seen light in series of lectures or talks over the years, including the Warfield Lectures in Oklahoma City; a lecture for a disability conference sponsored by Desiring God ministries; keynote addresses at undergraduate theology and philosophy conferences at University of Northwestern, St. Paul, Minnesota, and at Covenant College, Lookout Mountain, Tennessee; in sermons and Sunday school lessons at my home church, Spring Valley Presbyterian Church (now Christ Presbyterian Church), Roselle, Illinois; in the Christian Perspectives adult Sunday school class at Orchard Church, Arlington Heights, Illinois; and at the Chicago chapter of the C. S. Lewis Institute. I am also thankful to Wheaton College for granting me a sabbatical as I began work on this project.

For my wife, Cindy, no words are adequate.

A READER'S GUIDE

When we read texts that are meant to increase our understanding of the most important facets of our lives, good reading is always rereading. I've tried to write my text in such a way that it is as accessible as it can be, but some of its most important insights probably won't strike you your first time through the text.

I suggest that on a first and perhaps even second reading, you read only the main text and the footnotes. The footnotes, which are designated by small-letter superscripts like the one in this paragraph, will bolster your understanding of my text. During a second or third reading, please look up the Bible passages I've included. When I refer to biblical passages without quoting them, I put "see" before the reference to encourage you to look them up. There are a lot of those references because all of our theological claims should be backed up by Scripture. J. I. Packer has written that the "biblical references in my studies . . . are not . . . skippable; they are part of the argument, and are meant to be looked up."[a] The same goes here. As the psalmist prayed when he was suffering, "I am suffering terribly. O LORD, *revive me with your word!*" (Ps. 119:107 NET).

In quoting a lot of Scripture, my chapters include a lot of biblical poetry. A reader urged me to remove the poetry because many people find poetry so hard to understand that they may stop reading when they

---

a. J. I. Packer, *God's Words: Studies of Key Bible Themes* (Grand Rapids, MI: Baker, 1988), 7. Recently reprinted in a revised edition under the title *18 Words: The Most Important Words You Will Ever Know* (Ross-Shire, Scotland: Christian Focus, 2010).

encounter it. But about a third of the Bible is written as poetry, and so a lot of Scripture will remain closed to us if we don't learn how to read it. God inspired the Bible's authors to write poetry for good reasons and we need *all* of God's inspired word. If you find the poetry difficult, then read it aloud slowly several times. You'll begin to catch its rhythm and start understanding what it is saying. When we have learned how to read it, poetry is more meaningful than prose.

The endnotes, marked by superscript Arabic numerals, will help you think much more deeply about points in my text. Readers who have test-driven these books tell me that, once they have understood the main text, turning to the endnotes has enriched their understanding a lot. But please ignore the endnotes during at least your first reading.

This is the first of four volumes on Christian suffering, each of which will be identified as being part of a series entitled Suffering and the Christian Life. This volume introduces the topic and tries to offer suffering Christians some immediate aid by, among other things, showing that suffering is common in Scripture. We shouldn't be surprised when we suffer, and we should expect from what we find in Scripture that our God will help us through it. The second volume, which will appear in a year, answers the questions, Why do we suffer? and Why is there so much suffering? It places our suffering in the context of the full Christian story. The third volume shows that a thorough knowledge of Scripture is indispensable for healthy Christian life and then explores what Scripture tells us about the relationship between God's will and our suffering. It is meant to reassure you, if you are suffering, that nothing slips past God and he is always working for our good. The final volume will consider how suffering relates to the three Christian graces of faith, hope, and love. It closes by considering how we will regard our suffering in the afterlife.

Finally, I've chosen the English translation for each biblical passage that I think best combines readability and accuracy to the original languages.

NOTES

Chapter 1: When the Stars Disappear

1. *Webster's New Collegiate Dictionary*, 7th ed. (1971), s.v. "calamity."
2. "The name 'David' would appear to be connected with the Hebrew verbal root *d-w-d*, 'to love.' 'David,' then, would mean 'beloved,' presumably by Yahweh." David F. Payne in Geoffrey W. Bromiley, ed., *The International Standard Bible Encyclopedia*, rev. ed., 4 vols. (Grand Rapids, MI: Eerdmans, 1989), 1:871.
3. Henri Blocher, *Evil and the Cross: An Analytical Look at the Problem of Pain* (Grand Rapids, MI: Kregel, 1994), 9. Blocher's book is about the problem of evil and not just about the problem of Christian suffering. He believes the larger problem is insoluble, which leads him to observe that "the *problem* of evil . . . torments the human mind. It is a 'problem' in the original sense of the word, that of an obstacle thrown across our path, something that blocks our view, for it resists our unremitting efforts to *understand* it."

   I think the reasons why God has ordained specific Christians to suffer in specific ways may transcend our understanding, although his utter and complete goodness to each of us in ordaining what he does will be apparent in the life to come (see Rom. 8:28 and 2 Cor. 4:17).

   To say that God *has ordained* something means that he has so ordered or arranged events so that it comes about at the appropriate time. I will have much more to say about God's providential ordering of everything in my third volume.
4. I am using the phrase "God's Old Testament saints" to refer to God's Old Testament people. As C. John Collins explains in reference to Ps. 4:3, the Hebrew word that the ESV translates there as "the godly" is "the adjective form of 'steadfast love' (Hb. [*chesed*]). This term, variously rendered 'godly,' 'saint,' 'faithful one,' and 'holy one' in the Psalms, refers to those who have genuinely laid hold of God's steadfast love" (*ESV Study Bible*, ed. Wayne Grudem [Wheaton, IL: Crossway, 2008], 945). The New Testament enlarges the class to include God's New Testament people (see, e.g., Matt. 27:52 with Acts 9:13 and Rom. 1:7). I shall sometimes refer to all of those whom God has redeemed as "the saints."
5. Augustine, *Sermons*, vol. 9 (Hyde Park, NY: New City Press, 1994), 282 (Sermon 339, sec. 4).

6. Scripture licenses this metaphor in passages such as Ezek. 32:7–8; Joel 2:1–2, 10; 3:14–15; and Zeph. 1:14–16. The psalmists often likened their suffering to being in storms at sea, as we shall see.

7. More technically, getting our bearings in life involves understanding our lives as including a set or series of *narratives*—that is, a set or series of stories that orient us to life by enabling us to perceive series of events and actions as involving meaningful sequences. Some narratives are short (e.g., "When I went to the grocery store today, you'll never guess who I saw!") and others longer (e.g., "My high school and college years were quite eventful"). Christians believe God has created the world for a purpose and that he has a narrative that articulates how he will accomplish that purpose. They believe their particular stories should track God's narrative.

Of course, my use of the word *story* to refer to narratives does not imply that those narratives are untrue. I may, for instance, ask you, "What's your life story?" and expect you will (so far as you are able) tell me a true story about your life. In fact, you are obliged to tell as true a story as you can.

8. See 2 Cor. 11:16–12:10 for Paul's first-person chronicle of his sufferings and afflictions, including his thorn in the flesh. Paul Barnett explores in detail the place of suffering in Paul's life and ministry in his *The Second Epistle to the Corinthians*, New International Commentary on the New Testament (Grand Rapids, MI: Eerdmans, 1997).

Chapter 2: Suffering Saints

1. Why do we tend to feel this way? Part of the reason may be that we don't really notice profound suffering until after we have experienced it. Until then, it is as if there is no such thing.

The unreality of profound suffering for many of us means it can challenge our faith when we first confront it. When twenty-six people—including twenty first graders—were shot to death by a disturbed young man in Newtown, Connecticut, on December 14, 2012, his act seemed so evil that some pastors were asking on network television, "How could God allow this?" Their tone suggested they were doubting their faith. But then they had to be overlooking similar suffering in Scripture, such as Herod's slaughter of at least as many innocent children in Matt. 2:16–18. Matthew noted that Jeremiah had predicted that slaughter, which shows it didn't surprise God. And the fact that Matthew included it in his Gospel means that he didn't think it told against Christian faith. Indeed, the first Christians took the prediction's fulfillment by the actual tragic event to confirm that Jesus was God's own Son.

Of course, we should be appalled by such tragedies—"Rejoice with those who rejoice, weep with those who weep" (Rom. 12:15)—but their presence in Scripture should help us maintain our faith in the face of similar tragedies in our day.

2. Nothing in the book of Ruth confirms Naomi's sense that her suffering resulted from her sins, although it has been conjectured that it was sinful for Elimelech and Naomi to take their family out of Israel to Moab during the famine. The book, however, never explains why Naomi suffered as she did. We are aware only of the good that came from her suffering.

3. Many commentators interpret Naomi's claims at 1:13, 20–21 as involving her questioning God's goodness. I don't because (1) the fact that she set out for Israel while still grieving means that she still took the Lord to be her God (see 1:6–7); her heading for home suggests that she was not rebelling or running away from him. (2) Even in her desolation she commended her daughters-in-law to the Lord's loving care (see 1:8–9). (3) Ruth would not have identified so fully with Naomi, Naomi's people, and Naomi's God if Naomi had conveyed that her God was not good or was not to be obeyed (see 1:16–17). (4) Very soon after returning to Bethlehem, Naomi invoked the Lord's blessing on Boaz with the observation that God in his kindness had not forsaken the living (including herself) or the dead (see 2:20). And (5) since Naomi took her suffering as just punishment for some sin, she probably took the Almighty to be righteous in afflicting her. Her sense of her sinfulness may have made her feel that she had no ground for complaint (cf. Ezra 9:10–15 for a potential parallel). Consequently, I take Naomi's statements in 1:13, 20–21 as her merely reporting, rather than protesting or complaining about, what God had ordained for her. Yet even if the majority of commentators are right, Naomi's complaints would not threaten the points I will make about her in chap. 4.

4. For instance, adolescents sometimes declare, "I wish I had never been born!" even though onlookers know they are being shortsighted. Moreover, such overreactions are not limited to adolescents: Jonah reacted similarly (Jonah 4).

5. Job's symptoms suggest a kind of wasting disease like what strikes untreated HIV patients, including festering sores and scabs (see 7:5; 30:30a), fever (see 30:30b), excessive thinness (see 17:7b; 19:20), gaunt, death-like eyes (see 16:16), and constant, gnawing pain (see 30:17b). His appearance made everyone abhor him (see 19:13–19; 30:10). Scripture indicates that a disease like Job's could signify that God had cursed the sufferer (see Deut. 28:22, 35; Ps. 106:15). For more about what Job's symptoms could entail, see chap. 4, n. 17.

At least initially Job acquiesced to whatever God might send him (see 2:10). As his story unfolds, however, it shows how profound suffering can overwhelm even one whom the Old Testament identifies as a great hero of righteousness (see Ezek. 14:14, 20).

6. Some of Job's statements in chap. 9 (see, e.g., vv. 3, 16, 19) may seem to suggest otherwise. Yet even these claims don't falsify the trust that Job exhibits in chap. 23.

7. J. A. Thompson comments:

The call here to a life of celibacy is unique in the OT. In the ancient Near East, and therefore in Israel, a large family betokened divine blessing (Gen. 22:17; Ps. 127:3–4; etc.). Sterility and barrenness, on the other hand, were regarded as a curse (Gen. 30:1; 1 Sam. 1:6–8; etc.), and virginity was regarded as a cause for mourning (Judg. 11:37). An old Sumerian proverb curses celibacy. Hence it was altogether unusual for a young man in Israel like Jeremiah to remain unmarried. . . . The command to Jeremiah came in a peculiarly emphatic form. The negative used was *lō'* rather than the more usual *'al*. The use of *lō'* denotes something permanent and indicated that never, in any circumstances, was the prophet to marry. A similar usage occurs in the Ten Commandments. In a sense, Jeremiah was given his own special commandment. (*The Book of Jeremiah* [Grand Rapids, MI: Eerdmans, 1980], 403–4.)

Giving the Jewish perspective on marriage, Nahum M. Sarna notes:

> The idea here [at Gen. 2:18] is that man is recognized to be a social being. Celibacy is undesirable. Genesis Rabba 17:2 expresses this point as follows: "Whoever has no wife exists without goodness, without a helpmate, without joy, without blessing, without atonement . . . without well-being, without a full life; . . . indeed, such a one reduces the representation of the divine image [on earth]." (*The JPS Torah Commentary: Genesis* [Philadelphia: Jewish Publication Society, 1989], 21.)

8. Jeremiah probably expressed these "confessions" privately, for he, like the psalmist (see Ps. 73:15), would have been aware that to voice them publicly would tend to undermine others' faith. Gerhard von Rad observes that these passages "involve all the emotional conflicts brought on by [Jeremiah's] calling. We encounter here the whole gamut of human emotional problems: anxiety over shame, fear of failure, despair over one's ability to cope, doubts concerning articles of faith, loneliness, . . . disillusionment leading ultimately to hatred towards God. No feeling that can possibly come into a human heart is missing." Gerhard von Rad, "The Confessions of Jeremiah," in *Theodicy in the Old Testament*, ed. James L. Crenshaw (Philadelphia: Fortress, 1983), 97.

9. This passage has been interpreted in many ways, including some arguing that Jeremiah was not actually cursing the man who announced his birth (see, e.g., Peter C. Craigie, Page H. Kelley, and Joel F. Drinkard Jr., *Jeremiah 1–25*, Word Biblical Commentary [Dallas: Word, 1991], 277–78).

Derek Kidner thinks it expresses a "wild cry of pain" that involves some "extravagance" on Jeremiah's part, but one that gives us insight into "some other extremes of invective in Scripture" (Derek Kidner, *The Message of Jeremiah: Against Wind and Tide* [Downers Grove, IL: InterVarsity Press, 1987], 81). "For even if (which is unlikely) he genuinely wished a particular day of the year to become one of ill omen (14), he certainly could not have seriously consigned his father's friend to misery and death for not perpetrating a double murder (15–17)!" Kidner continues: "What these curses convey, therefore, is a state of mind, not a prosaic plea. The heightened language is not there to be analysed: it is there to bowl us over. Together with other tortured cries from him and his fellow sufferers, these raw wounds in Scripture remain lest we forget the sharpness of the age-long struggle, or the frailty of the finest overcomers" (81).

Given the intensification of his emotions prior to chap. 20, I think Jeremiah probably meant what he said. This passage then shows there is very little that God's saints may not entertain when they are suffering profoundly. His curse is especially shocking when we remember that he was not some loose talker and would have no doubt kept watch over his words. He would have known that we will be judged for our every loose word (see Prov. 10:19; Eccles. 5:2; Isa. 6:5). Yet, as we shall see, this did not preclude God's continuing to be gracious and merciful to him.

10. This valley, located directly south of Jerusalem, was the city dump. The New Testament Greek word *géenna*—sometimes transliterated as *Gehenna* and standing for the place of eternal punishment (see Mark 9:43–48)—is derived from abbreviating the Hebrew name for this valley, which reveals how it came to be viewed after God fulfilled Jeremiah's prophecy.

11. "The reference seems to be to the overthrow of all the ideas and intentions which the people carried out in the land in every department of their life" (Thompson, *Book of Jeremiah*, 450). In other words, God was going to destroy all the ordinary, everyday hopes of his apostate people. The stars by which they oriented their lives were to disappear.

12. See 20:1–2. We are told that Jeremiah was struck or beaten and put "in the stocks" (20:2), but it is unclear exactly what the Hebrew word "stocks" means. If its meaning follows its etymology—*mahpeketh* comes from a root involving something being wrenched or distorted—then it probably means that Jeremiah was tortured. Since this appears to be the first time he was physically abused for speaking the prophetic word, it seems to have triggered his violent emotional reaction.

13. Moses confronted God somewhat similarly when he thought God was causing the Israelites grief by not rescuing them from Pharaoh's wrath (see Ex. 5:22–23). Commenting on Jer. 20:7–10, William L. Holladay notes:

> Verse 7a is unique, an accusation of deception leveled at Yahweh. There are many complaints in the Psalms that Yahweh has taken the psalmist to the gates of Sheol or the like (for example, Ps 88:7), but there is no parallel for this accusation. . . . Verse 7b is a more conventional statement, the complaint that the suppliant is the cause of derision (Pss. 22:8; 44:14–15; 79:4); but vv 8–9 connect that derision with the word of Yahweh, and that is new. (William L. Holladay, *Jeremiah 1: A Commentary on the Book of the Prophet Jeremiah, Chapters 1–25* [Philadelphia: Fortress, 1986], 551.)

Yet Jeremiah's accusations in v. 7 may be even darker. The Hebrew words *patah* (translated as "deceived" in the first line) and *chazaq* (translated as "overpowered" in the second) have sexual overtones—*patah* sometimes refers to someone who has been *seduced* (see Ex. 22:16; Judg. 16:5) and *chazaq* sometimes indicates that someone has been raped (see Deut. 22:25; 2 Sam. 13:11, 14; cf. Prov. 7:13). This led the great Jewish biblical scholar Abraham J. Heschel to translate the verse as, "O Lord, Thou hast seduced me, / And I am seduced; / Thou hast raped me / And I am overcome" (Abraham J. Heschel, *The Prophets: An Introduction* [New York: Harper & Row, 1969], 113).

In attempting to make sense of this sort of accusation against God, J. A. Thompson says:

> Jeremiah seems to be saying that he had understood his relationship to Yahweh to be something like a marriage bond but it was

now clear that he had been deceived, enticed by Yahweh, who had used him and tossed him aside. The language verges on the blasphemous. . . . But more than that, Yahweh had *laid hold on* ("overpowered" . . .) him and had prevailed over him. . . . Perhaps the sense is, "you forced me," carrying on the metaphor of seduction. (Thompson, *Book of Jeremiah*, 459.)

Holladay finds Jeremiah using marriage images for his relationship with God in 15:16 and 20:11 (see Holladay, *Jeremiah 1*, 458–59, 549–50). He may be right that Jeremiah's "acceptance of the call to be a messenger of Yahweh's word gave him the delight analogous to that in marriage" (459). Evidence for such an interpretation may include Jeremiah's claim at 15:16 that when he found God's words, he devoured them as his heart's joy and delight because he took himself to be called by God's name. This parallels how lovers read letters from their beloveds.

14. In his *At the Mind's Limits: Contemplations by a Survivor on Auschwitz and Its Realities* (Bloomington: Indiana University Press, 1980), Jean Améry observes that with the very first blow a prisoner receives in custody, he loses his trust in the world, including his trust that "the other person will spare me—more precisely stated, that he will respect my physical, and with it also my metaphysical, being" (28; see 24–29). I think Jeremiah felt something like what Améry describes after Pashhur struck him or had him beaten (see 20:2, where *nakah* can mean either strike or beat), as long as we substitute "trust in God" for "trust in the world."

15. Gerhard von Rad notes that in addition to Jeremiah's explicit resolution in 20:9, his confession in 15:16–18 included a desire "to withdraw from his prophetic office" and "become a citizen among citizens," and that, at 20:8, he desired that "God should find himself another person" (von Rad, "The Confessions of Jeremiah," 90, 94).

16. J. R. Soza observes:

> Jeremiah is called . . . to identify with God in his being obliged to forgo marriage and children so as to symbolize the barrenness of a land under judgment (16:1–4). God signifies the complete end of his relationship with Israel by his representative prophet's not having a wife or bearing children. Natural life as the Israelites know it is becoming extinct. Jeremiah himself is called to extinction. By his life he symbolizes the death of his people. . . . Jeremiah's bachelorhood . . . is so unusual among the Jews that the OT has no word for bachelor, and it undoubtedly reinforces questions about him." (*New Dictionary of Biblical Theology*, ed. Brian S. Rosner, T. Desmond Alexander, et al. [Downers Grove, IL: InterVarsity Press, 2000], s.v. "Jeremiah.")

Jeremiah's bachelorhood may have prompted his countrymen to suspect he was homosexual.

17. See 17:15–18. Jeremiah's request in v. 18, "Let those be put to shame who persecute me, but let me not be put to shame; let them be dismayed, but let me not

be dismayed; bring upon them the day of disaster; destroy them with double destruction!" seems to be a response to his opponents' taunt in v. 15: "Where is the word of the LORD? Let it come!" Jeremiah's plea "LORD, don't terrorize me!" in v. 17 (NLT) may very well express his fear that despite the fact that he has not shirked his prophetic task and has spoken all and only what God commanded (see v. 16), perhaps his words would indeed go unfulfilled.

Jeremiah probably knew that God had enticed King Ahab to his death by sending a lying spirit into the mouths of all of Ahab's prophets (see 1 Kings 22:13–23), which may have stoked his suspicions.

18. Gerhard von Rad, *Old Testament Theology*, vol. 2, *The Theology of Israel's Prophetic Traditions* (New York: Harper & Row, 1965), 205. I am echoing von Rad's observations in this paragraph. We shall see that often the worst part of profound suffering is that we can't make sense of it because we can't trace God's good hand in it. This is what Jeremiah's confessions convey.

19. Kidner notes that in Jeremiah's declaration in v. 13, "Sing to the LORD; praise the LORD! For he has delivered the life of the needy from the hand of evildoers," the phrase "the needy" is singular, signifying that Jeremiah was referring specifically to his own deliverance from the stocks (Kidner, *Message of Jeremiah*, 80).

Chapter 3: Breathing Lessons

1. See, e.g., Dietrich Bonhoeffer's little classic *Psalms: The Prayer Book of the Bible* (Minneapolis: Augsburg, 1970) and Eugene H. Peterson's *Answering God: The Psalms as Tools for Prayer* (New York: HarperCollins, 1989).

2. Old Testament prayer characteristically calls upon God as "LORD"—in other words, as Yahweh, which is so to speak God's personal name—and thus addresses him person to person (see Gen. 4:26; Deut. 4:7).

3. Peterson writes, "Our habit is to talk about God, not to him. We love discussing God. The Psalms resist these discussions. They are not provided to teach us about God but to train us in responding to him." This is the posture of prayer and so, Peterson concludes, "we don't learn the Psalms until we are praying them" (Peterson, *Answering God*, 12). Psalm 39 is a striking example of this. It is intriguing to think how much Christian talk about suffering would be transformed if we followed David's lead in this psalm of addressing God directly as "LORD" and "you."

4. See, e.g., Ps. 150:1–2: "Praise the LORD! Praise God in his sanctuary; praise him in his mighty heavens! Praise him for his mighty deeds; praise him according to his excellent greatness!" This is third-person language that refers to God without addressing him directly. Pss. 1; 2; 11; 14; 24; 29; 34; 37; 46; 47; 49; 50; 53; 78; 81; 87; 91; 95; 96; 98; 100; 103; 105; 107; 110–14; 117; 121; 122; 124; 127–29; 133; 134; 136; and 146–150 refer to God exclusively in the third person.

5. It is a bit unclear which psalms should be classified as laments, since some psalms contain lament-like pleas without perhaps actually being laments (see, e.g., Pss. 40; 41; 94). Psalms 3; 4; 5; 6; 7; 9–10 (9–10 together form an incomplete acrostic and so probably should be read as one psalm); 12; 13; 17; 22; 25; 26; 28; 31; 35; 38; 39; 42–43 (these two psalms form a single prayer); 44; 51; 52;

54; 55; 56; 57; 58; 59; 60; 61; 62; 63; 64; 69; 70; 71; 74; 77; 79; 80; 83; 85; 86; 88; 89; 90; 102; 108; 109; 120; 123; 130; 137; 140; 141; 142; 143; and 144 are usually classified as laments. Most of these are *individual* laments—e.g., "Deliver *me*, O Lord, from evil men; preserve *me* from violent men" (Ps. 140:1)—although some are *community* laments, e.g., "By the waters of Babylon, there *we* sat down and wept, when *we* remembered Zion" (Ps. 137:1).

6. Eugene Peterson writes that "the language of prayer is forged in the crucible of trouble," noting:

> "O Lord, how many are my foes!" is . . . the first sentence in the first prayer in the Psalms (3:1). Brief, urgent, frightened words—a person in trouble, crying out to God for help. The language is personal, direct, desperate. This is the language of prayer: men and women calling out their trouble—pain, guilt, doubt, despair—to God. Their lives are threatened. If they don't get help they will be dead, or diminished to some critical degree. (Peterson, *Answering God*, 35.)

Prayer, he observes:

> occurs primarily at one level, the personal, and for one purpose, salvation. The human condition teeters on the edge of disaster. Human beings are in trouble most of the time. Those who don't know they are in trouble are in the worst trouble. Prayer is the language of the people who are in trouble and know it, and who believe or hope that God can get them out. As prayer is practiced, it moves into other levels and develops other forms, but trouble—being in the wrong, being in danger, realizing that the foes are too many for us to handle—is the basic provocation for prayer. . . . The recipe for obeying St. Paul's "Pray without ceasing" is . . . a watchful recognition of the trouble we are in. (Peterson, *Answering God*, 36–37.)

7. 2 Sam. 7:1–17 records God's pledge to David to establish the throne of his descendants forever, with Ps. 2:7–8 alluding to this pledge. Heb. 1:5 puts Ps. 2:7 and 2 Sam. 7:14 together as ultimately referring to our Lord. Peterson's chapter on the first two psalms is revelatory (see Peterson, *Answering God*, 23–32).

8. All but the first two psalms in book 1 of the Psalms (that is, Pss. 3–41) have a heading referring to David. The headings do not, as Michael Wilcock notes, "necessarily mean 'by David'; they could 'belong to' him in various other ways (about him; for his use; dedicated to him, in a collection under his name; and so on). But there is generally no strong reason why it should not mean authorship, and in some cases—for example, Psalm 18—it clearly does" (Michael Wilcock, *The Message of Psalms 1–72*, The Bible Speaks Today [Nottingham, UK: Inter-Varsity Press, 2001], 25). Following the common New Testament practice, I will refer to the psalms having the word "David" in their titles as David's psalms (see Matt. 22:43, 45; Acts 2:25).

9. Derek Kidner notes that David's world, as exemplified in vv. 3 and 4 of Ps. 13, had two poles: "God, but for whom life would be insupportable, and the enemy,

because of whom any wavering . . . must be unthinkable. Awareness of God and the enemy," he continues, "is virtually the hallmark of every psalm of David; the positive and negative charge which produced the driving-force of his best years" (Derek Kidner, *Psalms 1–72* [Leicester, England: Inter-Varsity Press, 1973], 77–78). Similarly, Jesus chose Paul to spread the gospel and suffer *much* for his sake (see Acts 9:10–16). Life's troubles should prompt us to think about God and reflect on his word in life-giving ways.

10. Claus Westermann stresses that biblical prayer responds to God's initiatives:

    One side of what takes place between God and humanity is response. Contrary to the opinion that prayer and offering are works initiated by humans, the Old Testament understands them both as response. There would be neither cult nor prayer if it were not for the acts and words of God. However, it must be said with equal emphasis that the acts and words of God cannot remain unanswered. God acts and speaks in order to elicit a response, both in action and in speech. What happens in the Old Testament has the form of dialogue. A typical example from the Old Testament is the first commandment in its dialogue structure "I-thou." Another example is the double meaning of the verb *berek*, which in the direction from God to man means "to bless," and in the reverse direction "to praise." A typical example from the New Testament is Luke 1–2, where what happens between God and humanity is accompanied at every point by human response, as shown in the songs of praise running through [these chapters]. (Claus Westermann, *Elements of Old Testament Theology*, trans. Douglas W. Stott [Atlanta: John Knox, 1982], 153.)

11. See Gen. 1:28 for what is called "the creation mandate" and 2:16–17 for the first commandment. (The various elements of the so-called creation mandate are all framed as imperatives, so it is really a command, too.)

12. The psalmists remembered what God had said to their first ancestor, Abraham:

    The Lord said to Abraham, "Why did Sarah laugh and say, 'Shall I indeed bear a child, now that I am old?' *Is anything too hard for the Lord?* At the appointed time I will return to you, about this time next year, and Sarah shall have a son." . . . [And the] Lord visited Sarah as he had said, and the Lord did to Sarah as he had promised. And Sarah conceived and bore Abraham a son in his old age at the time of which God had spoken to him. (Gen. 18:13–14; 21:1–2; cf. Job 42:1–2 and Jer. 32:17, 27.)

13. See Ps. 71, especially vv. 5–6, 9, 15, 17–21. Echoes of other psalms and the lack of a clear structure suggest this psalm was written in old age. See Wilcock, *Message of Psalms 1–72*, 246.

14. J. I. Packer notes:

    God declared [his] name to Moses when he spoke to him out of the thornbush that burned steadily without being burned up. God began by identifying himself as the God who had committed himself in covenant to the patriarchs (cf. Gen. 17:1–14); then, when Moses asked him what he might tell the people that this God's name was (for the ancient assumption was that prayer would be heard only if you named its addressee correctly), God first said "I am who I am" (or, "I will be what I will be"), then shortened it to "I am," and finally called himself "the LORD (Hebrew *Yahweh*, a name sounding like 'I am' in Hebrew), the God of your fathers" (Ex. 3:6, 13–16). The name in all its forms proclaims his eternal, self-sustaining, self-determining, sovereign reality—that supernatural mode of existence that the sign of the burning bush had signified. The bush, we might say, was God's three-dimensional illustration of his own inexhaustible life. "This is my name forever," he said—that is, God's people should always think of him as the living, reigning, potent, unfettered and undiminished king that the burning bush showed him to be (Ex. 3:15).

Later (Ex. 33:18–34:7) Moses asks to see God's "glory" (adorable self-display), and in reply God did "proclaim his name" thus: "The Lord, the Lord, the compassionate and gracious God, slow to anger, abounding in love and faithfulness, maintaining love to thousands, and forgiving wickedness, rebellion and sin. Yet he does not leave the guilty unpunished . . ." At the burning bush God had answered the question, In what way does God exist? Here he answers the question, In what way does God behave? This foundational announcement of his moral character is often echoed in later Scriptures (Neh. 9:17; Ps. 86:15; Joel 2:13; Jonah 4:2). It is all part of his "name," that is, his disclosure of his nature, for which he is to be adored forever. (J. I. Packer, *Concise Theology: A Guide to Historic Christian Beliefs* [Wheaton, IL: Tyndale, 1993], 23–25.)

15. When God promised David that he would establish David's throne forever, David responded by asking God to keep his word, noting that his courage to pray that God would do as he had promised rested on what God had just revealed to him (see 2 Sam. 7:11, 16, 25, 27).

16. R. W. L. Moberly notes that "since Israel elsewhere confesses that the Lord in his care for Israel 'will neither slumber nor sleep' ([Ps.] 121:4), and Elijah mocks the prophets of Baal that their god who is no God 'is maybe sleeping and must be awakened' (1 Kgs 18:27), this is language that jars, and is presumably meant to jar, with Israel's official faith. In the expression of deep pain, the finer nuances of theological discourse may need to be left aside" ("Psalms: Theology of," in *New International Dictionary of Old Testament Theology and Exegesis*, ed. Willem A. VanGemeren, 5 vols. [Grand Rapids, MI: Zondervan, 1997], 4:880).

Kidner perceptively notes that "although [v. 23's] picture of the sleeping Lord may seem naïve to us, it was acted out in the New Testament, to teach a lesson which we still find relevant: *cf.* verse 23 with Mark 4:38" (Kidner, *Psalms 1–72*, 170).

17. Moberly defines biblical lament as "turning to God in prayer in times of distress." He then sets the biblical laments in the more general context of Old Testament faith:

> Although the OT constantly stresses the importance of [trust, faith, and obedience] as characterizing the true human response to God, the general canonical presentation is such that these are not to be conceived in any simplistic way, as though life were essentially a matter of "obeying orders." Rather, there is a recurrent portrayal of life under God as containing space for dialogue with God, with room for question and answer. Obedience to God is to be set in the context of an intelligent relationship and not be mindless. (Moberly, "Psalms, Theology of," 876.)

18. Pss. 44 and 89 are community laments that "show every sign of being carefully crafted compositions to present the paradox of God's apparent absence in the life of faith" (Moberly, "Psalms: Theology of," 880). Ps. 44 turns bleak at v. 9, even as it insists, both before and after (see vv. 4–8, 17–18), that God's people have done nothing to deserve harsh treatment. In vv. 34–37 of Ps. 89 we find, Moberly notes, "the strongest and most emphatic commitment ascribed to God in the whole [Old Testament]." Up to this point, "we have a hymn to the God of sovereign power, who is noted for his faithfulness and who has made an absolute commitment to be faithful to the house of David" (881). Yet starting with v. 38, the current situation is depicted, "which stands in complete opposition to what had been promised. 'I will crush his foes before him' (v. 23) has become 'You have exalted the right hand of his foes' (v. 42), and 'I will not violate my covenant' (v. 34) has become 'You have renounced the covenant' (v. 39). The difference between the absolute promise and what has actually happened could not be starker" (881). The psalm's final section "consists of a cry to the Lord, appealing, like Ps 44, to the Lord's [steadfast love] . . . , but receiving no answer or word of assurance" (881). The psalm's final verse—"Blessed be the Lord forever! Amen and Amen"—marks the end of the third book of the Psalter and so simply follows the pattern of praise of the doxologies found at the end of each of its books.

    Both psalms "pose the theological problem of the conflict between Israel's recognized faith in God and the agonizingly disappointing situations that may actually arise (and presumably [do] arise on numerous occasions)" (882). "It is essential," Moberly notes, "to the understanding of each psalm that the tension be maintained between its conflicting elements, the formal confession of faith and the problematic circumstances. . . . The conflict may be agonizing and lacking resolution, yet it is characteristic of the psalmist that the conflict must be faced and endured, if faith is to be genuine and avoid either unreality or despair" (882).

19. Thompson renders the verse like this:

> O Lord, thou art in the right
> When I dispute with thee.
> Yet there are cases I would argue with thee.

Why does the way of wicked men succeed?
Why are all treacherous men at ease?

(Thompson's second-person singular *thous* and *thees* emphasize that this prayer is addressed to God alone.) He then comments:

In 12:1–6 we have one of Jeremiah's "confessions," a brief self-reve-lation in which a man lays bare some of his own deep questionings and intimate feelings. . . . The problem raised is the age-old ques-tion of why the wicked should flourish. They were God's creatures. It lay in his power to bring them to judgment. But they pursued their evil ways unchecked and caused innocent men to suffer. Why, for example, should Jeremiah, God's servant, called to declare his word to disobedient Israel, be subjected to the treacherous plots of the men of his own village? Like Job and some of the psalmists Jer-emiah believed in God and stood under his sovereignty but found his ways hard to comprehend. There is no question that Yahweh is in the right. . . . The righteous man was the man who was faithful to all his obligations of whatever kind. . . . No legal complaint can be brought against Yahweh since he is innocent of all charges. Yet there were some specific cases . . . of "right" that Jeremiah wished to discuss, namely, cases where the wicked prosper. (Thompson, *Book of Jeremiah*, 352–52.)

Job also desired to take his case directly to God (see Job 10; 13:3, 13–15; and 31:35–37) even as he also trusted in God's righteousness (see 23:1–7). Pss. 10 and 73 express similar perplexities.

20. Patrick D. Miller observes that the language the psalms use to express distress from enemies "is stereotypical and imaginative, but it can hardly be understood apart from the real presence of such hostile forces" (Patrick D. Miller, *They Cried to the Lord: The Form and Theology of Biblical Prayer* [Minneapolis: For-tress, 1994], 105). He notes more generally:

It is characteristic of the psalmic prayers for help . . . that they are prayed in extremis, where life is perceived as in the balance, and only the protection or help of God can "preserve my life." . . . Sometimes the imagery and language suggesting the threat of death represent the powerful suffering of one whose actual life may not be threatened but who experiences life as so on the brink that the cry "Save my life" is authentic expression of where the sufferer really is. (106.)

In other words, sometimes the psalmists needed hyperbole in order to be able to express as accurately as they could what they were actually feeling.

21. Ps. 88 is unique among the personal laments in never expressing any hope or confidence that God will deliver the psalmist. As Moberly says, it "stands as a kind of boundary marker in the life of faith, a reminder that a sense of being forsaken by God can be both overwhelming and unrelieved" (Moberly, "Psalms: Theology of," 880).

22. Much of the horror of David's situation involved his enemies insinuating that no matter who God was and what he had done for his people in the past (depicted by the "Yet you" of vv. 3–5), he was not going to do the same for David now (see v. 8). David countered those insinuations with the "Yet you" of vv. 9–10. I assume David penned Ps. 22 in response to some crushingly horrendous experience. We can't, however, link it to any particular incident in his life and, in fact, as Derek Kidner observes, because it describes an execution, "the language of the psalm defies a [natural] explanation," since David wouldn't have survived to write it. Indeed, some of its verses, such as 16–18, had to await our Lord's scourging and crucifixion "to unfold their meaning with any clarity" (Kidner, *Psalms 1–72*, 105, 107).

23. With community laments, the vow to praise and actual praise are usually missing, although they often express trust and confidence in God and what he will do.

24. See the "Yet . . . you" and the "Yet you" at the beginnings of vv. 3 and 9 in Ps. 22, above; for a "But you," see 102:12. For "But I" where it signals a move to confidence and praise, see Pss. 13:5; 31:14; 71:14; and for an implicit "[But] I," see 27:13.

25. Regarding the psalmist's declaration that "since my youth, God, you have taught me, and to this day I declare your marvelous deeds. Even when I am old and gray, do not forsake me, my God, till I declare your power to the next generation, your mighty acts to all who are to come" (Ps. 71:17–18 NIV), Wilcock writes: "It goes without saying that our psalmist does not *declare [God's] marvellous deeds* (v. 17) because he likes the sound of his own voice. He speaks so that others may hear; he sings so that they may join in. Specifically, he says, *I declare your power to the next generation* (v. 18). There is no shadow of doubt in his mind that God's great acts in the past are meant to benefit the people of the future. The notion that the mere passage of time renders Bible truth obsolete is one of the more idiotic of modern ideas. . . . There is nothing more relevant *to all who are to come* (v. 18) than the vital proclamation of what God did in Bible times, and of the truth that that embodies. He is, after all, the incomparable God. *Who, O God, is like you?* says verse 19" (Wilcock, *Message of Psalms 1–72*, 248–49; emphasis original).

Chapter 4: The Rest of Their Stories

1. C. S. Lewis wrote: "Christianity . . . makes world-history in its entirety a single, transcendentally significant, story with a well-defined plot pivoted on Creation, Fall, Redemption, and Judgment" (C. S. Lewis, *The Discarded Image: An Introduction to Medieval and Renaissance Literature* [Cambridge, UK: Cambridge University Press, 1970], 194). *Judgment* takes place at the beginning of consummation and determines whether someone will experience what the Scottish Puritan Thomas Boston called "Consummate Happiness or Misery." The subtitle to Boston's *Human Nature in Its Fourfold State* (published in 1720) specified the four stages or states as, first, Primitive Integrity, then Entire Depravity, then Begun Recovery, and finally Consummate Happiness or Misery.

2. R. W. L. Moberly, "Psalms: Theology of," in *New International Dictionary of Old Testament Theology and Exegesis*, ed. Willem A. VanGemeren, 5 vols. (Grand Rapids, MI: Zondervan, 1997), 4:879; emphasis added. Earlier in the same piece he observes that "the Old Testament offers some striking portrayals of the possibly problematic nature of life under God" that establish that "coping with disappointment and speaking to God about it is . . . an integral part of the life of faith" (877–78). This means, he ultimately concludes, that "instead of the problems of the life of faith being put on one side, as though worship should really be just a matter of praise and thanksgiving, these problems are made central to the very act of prayer and worship" (879).

3. Here's the picture: David's enemies, whom he mentioned in v. 5, were often pursuing him and trying to hunt him down—and yet their pursuit was not everlasting, although God's *chesed* is. When all is said and done, only God's *chesed* will have endured throughout our lives and into the *eschaton*. God's *chesed* is, literally, unyielding and relentless. As Kidner puts the point of v. 6: "With God [the] qualities [of goodness and steadfast love] are not merely solid and dependable, but vigorous—for to *follow*"—as the Hebrew word for *pursue* has traditionally been translated—"does not mean here to bring up the rear but to pursue, as surely as [God's] judgments pursue the wicked (83:15)." Derek Kidner, *Psalms 1–72* (Leicester, England: Inter-Varsity Press, 1973), 112.

4. Daniel I. Block, *Judges and Ruth*, New American Commentary, vol. 6 (Nashville: B&H, 1999), 605.

5. D. A. Baer and R. P. Gordon write: "In the Psalms, both God and human worshipers describe God's [*chesed*] as everlasting. . . . In addition, one finds the related affirmation that God's [*chesed*] will be sung about forever, which is an oblique way of suggesting that his love itself will not end. This diversity of expression coalesces in a refrain that rumbles exuberantly through a wide range of texts: 'The Lord is good, his [*chesed*] endures forever.' . . . One subtext to the plot of God's eternal [*chesed*] is his self-binding oath or promise to provide such beneficence into the future. Several texts (e.g., Deut 7:12; Mic 7:20) invoke this promise as encouragement, even as others (cf. Ps 25:7; 89:49 [50]; 119:41, 76) find it urgent to remind God of his obligation." D. A. Baer and R. P. Gordon, "chesed," in *The New International Dictionary of Old Testament Theology and Exegesis*, ed. Willem VanGemeren (Grand Rapids, MI: Zondervan, 1997), 2:210.

6. Derek Kidner, *Psalms 73–150* (London: Inter-Varsity Press, 1975), 311.

7. Baer and Gordon, "chesed," 208–9.

8. Some translations attempt to preserve the Hebrew wordplay in v. 20 by translating the verse as "Call me Mara, for Shaddai has marred me bitterly" (JB) or "Call me Mara, for the Almighty has cruelly marred me" (Moffatt), as F. B. Huey Jr. notes in his commentary on Ruth (*Deuteronomy, Joshua, Judges, Ruth, 1 and 2 Samuel*, vol. 3, Expositor's Bible Commentary, ed. Frank E. Gaebelein [Grand Rapids, MI: Zondervan, 1992], 526). This feature of the Hebrew text confirms that Naomi took her sufferings to have been ordained by God.

9. The Hebrew adjective *ṭôb*, here translated as "better," carries overtones of pleasantness. Israelites considered a family of seven sons to be the ideal of a full, satisfying family life (see 1 Sam. 2:5).

10. See Frederic W. Bush, *Ruth, Esther*, Word Biblical Commentary, vol. 9 (Dallas: Word, 1996), 52.

11. Robert L. Hubbard Jr. emphasizes that while the practice of *chesed* is presented in Ruth as the Israelite ideal, it requires extraordinary commitment. It goes beyond what is expected. Those who don't practice *chesed*—such as when Naomi's unnamed relative decides not to redeem her field because his inheritance would be endangered by marrying Ruth (4:1–6)—aren't doing anything wrong, but in doing only what is expected, they aren't practicing *chesed*. Those who, like Ruth and Boaz, practice *chesed* become Israelite role models (see Robert L. Hubbard Jr., *The Book of Ruth* [Grand Rapids, MI: Eerdmans, 1988], 72–73).
    This may seem to suggest that *chesed* is supererogatory—in other words, above and beyond the call of duty. But Mic. 6:8 says otherwise: "He has told you, O man, what is good; and what does the LORD require of you but to do justice, and to love kindness [*chesed*], and to walk humbly with your God?" Paradoxically, *chesed* is required of the Lord's people!

12. Naomi attributed *chesed* to Ruth and her sister in v. 8: "May the Lord deal kindly [*chesed*] with you, as you have dealt with the dead and with me." At 1:14 we are told that Ruth "clung to" Naomi in refusing to leave her and, as Huey notes, the Hebrew word for *clung to* "elsewhere expresses the ideal closeness that can be experienced in a marriage relationship (Gen. 2:24; 1 Kings 11:2)" (Huey, *Ruth*, Expositor's Bible Commentary, 522). Ruth's *chesed* to Naomi was manifested in a lifelong, until-death-do-us-part commitment (see v. 17). Huey also suggests that "by first naming the people and then God [in her declaration in v. 16], Ruth revealed that she could not relate to God apart from his people" (524).
    At 2:20 Naomi counts Boaz's kindness to Ruth as God's kindness to her family: "And Naomi said to her daughter-in-law, 'May he be blessed by the Lord, whose kindness [*chesed*] has not forsaken the living or the dead!'"

13. "No one in the book demands of God that he meet his/her needs. . . . On the contrary, true [*chesed*] is expressed by concern for the welfare of others. In the story this concern is expressed by loving actions that promote the next person's well-being and by verbal expressions of prayer for the next person. . . . It is striking that no one in the book prays for a resolution of his own crisis. In each case a person prays that Yahweh would bless someone else. This is a mark of *chesed*" (Block, *Judges and Ruth*, 611–13).
    My third chapter showed that we must pray for ourselves. Such prayers are crucial to our communication and communion with God and thus to sustaining our spiritual lives. And, indeed, the mere fact that such prayers are not found in the book of Ruth does not mean they weren't made. Yet their absence in the book of Ruth emphasizes that we sometimes ought to be more concerned about the well-being of others than about our own well-being.

14. After Ruth proposed to Boaz at night on the threshing floor, he declared, "May you be blessed by the LORD, my daughter. You have made this last kindness

[*chesed*] greater than the first in that you have not gone after young men, whether poor or rich" (3:10). The NLT translates *chesed* here as "family loyalty," which emphasizes that Ruth was thinking about Naomi more than herself.

15. This repayment often occurs during our earthly lifetimes, although God has not promised it will. For the general principle see 2 Sam. 22:26 and Prov. 19:17. For its ultimate and sure eschatological fulfillment, see Matt. 5:7; 25:31–46 and Luke 6:37–38.

16. While Naomi seems to express utter hopelessness regarding herself at 1:11–13, her remark to Ruth at 2:20—"And Naomi said to her daughter-in-law, 'May he be blessed by the LORD, whose kindness [*chesed*] has not forsaken the living or the dead!'"—shows that she still had some hope based in her trust in the character of Israel's God.

17. Job's social ostracism is detailed at 19:13–22 and 30:1, 9–15. In Leviticus, boils like Job's required the priest to declare the sufferer unclean. Persons with them had to "wear torn clothes, let their hair be unkempt, cover the lower part of their face, and cry out, 'Unclean! Unclean!'" (Lev. 13:45 NIV). They also had to live alone, outside the Israelite camp (see 13:46). Since we don't know when the book of Job was written, we don't know if its author was aware of these passages. Yet they show that in the ancient world a condition such as Job's was considered grave, required the sufferer's isolation, and was likely to imply judgment by God.

18. For Job's grief and confusion, see, e.g., 4:2–5; 8:2; 11:2–6; 15:2–6, 11–13. His suffering made him loquacious. For his friends' mercilessness, see 4:7–8, 17–19; 8:3–6; and especially 11:6—"Know . . . that God exacts of you less than your guilt deserves"—with 11:13–20.

19. John E. Hartley says:

> Job directly charges his friends with dealing treacherously with him. . . . He acknowledges a close relationship with his comforters, calling them friends and brothers [see 6:14–15]. The word *brothers* . . . and the term *loyal love* or *fidelity* (*chesed*, v. 14a) indicate that there probably existed an official bond or covenant between Job and these comforters (cf. 1 Sam. 20:8, 14–15 [with Job 2:11]). Their pact certainly included friendship and mutual support. Thus Job accuses his partners of failing to fulfill the obligations of their covenant relationship. (John E. Hartley, *The Book of Job*, 2nd ed. [Grand Rapids, MI: Eerdmans, 1988], 135–36.)

Tremper Longman III comments:

> In 6:14–30 Job expresses disappointment, even disgust, at the lack of support that his friends give him in the midst of his suffering. Indeed, they have intensified his pain rather than mitigating it. Job's words remind us of the importance of relationships in the midst of suffering.
>
> It is tempting to think that the biblical view is that all one needs is God to make one's way in a difficult world, but this view is undermined as early as Gen. 2:4b–25. In this second creation

account, God creates Adam first. Adam is in a harmonious relationship with God. He lives in Eden, paradise. One would think he has everything, but God knows better and says, "It is not good that the man should be alone" (Gen. 2:18 NRSV). If this is true in Eden, how much more so in the world after the fall. (Tremper Longman III, *Job*, Baker Commentary on the Old Testament Wisdom and Psalms [Grand Rapids, MI: Baker Academic, 2012], 150–52.)

20. A self-imprecatory curse calls down judgment on oneself if one's claims are untrue. See Job 31:16–17, 19–22 for one of Job's curses.

21. In addition to telling Job that Job's understanding of what he was doing was profoundly offtrack ("Who is this that obscures my plans with words without knowledge?" [38:2 NIV]), God challenged Job to answer questions about creation to make clear that Job was ignorant of the biblical story's beginning as well as about its middle and end.

    Isa. 46:9–11 asserts God's exclusive knowledge of the world's whole story: "I am God, and there is no other; I am God, and there is none like me, declaring the end from the beginning and from ancient times things not yet done, saying, 'My counsel shall stand, and I will accomplish all my purpose,' calling a bird of prey from the east, the man of my counsel from a far country. I have spoken, and I will bring it to pass; I have purposed, and I will do it." His knowledge of all the details is affirmed in such passages as Ps. 139 and Matt. 10:28–31.

22. D. A. Carson comments regarding Job's struggles:

    > Job's speeches are the anguish of a man who knows God, who wants to know him better, who never once doubts the existence of God, who remains convinced, at bottom, of the justice of God— but who cannot make sense of these entrenched beliefs in the light of his own experience. (D. A. Carson, *How Long, O Lord? Reflections on Suffering and Evil* [Grand Rapids, MI: Baker, 1990], 166.)

    In other words, Job couldn't tell himself a coherent, satisfying story. This is not the posture of someone who is denying God. Job was simply seeking answers.

23. Yet God did not deceive Jeremiah, for while his actual experience of virtually universal opposition to himself as God's prophet proved psychologically overwhelming, God had told him when he first called him that he would face such opposition (1:18–19). This opposition amounted to Jeremiah's being denied *chesed* by nearly all of his fellow Israelites.

24. Paul R. House, in *ESV Study Bible*, ed. Wayne Grudem (Wheaton, IL: Crossway, 2008), 1363. See my comments from Jean Améry's *At the Mind's Limits* in chap. 2, n. 14.

25. Most commentators agree with Derek Kidner that after Jeremiah's "wild cry of pain" found at the end of chap. 20, he went on "to his worst ordeals with never a hesitation or a word of doubt" (Derek Kidner, *The Message of Jeremiah: Against Wind and Tide* [Downers Grove, IL: InterVarsity Press, 1987], 81). Kidner adds that "if ever one's morale as a servant of God touches rock-bottom, we may reflect that Jeremiah has been there before, and has survived" (80).

26. Job 42:12. Read vv. 10–17 to get the full picture. Of course, Job's grief from the loss of his first ten children surely never completely ceased, yet the blessings depicted in his book's final chapter falsify his despairing claim that his eye would never again see good.

27. I am quoting from the Collect for "The Second Sunday in Advent" from the Anglican *Book of Common Prayer*:

> Blessed Lord, who hast caused all holy Scriptures to be written for our learning: Grant that we may in such wise hear them, read, mark, learn, and inwardly digest them, that by patience and comfort of thy holy Word, we may embrace and ever hold fast the blessed hope of everlasting life, which thou hast given us in our Saviour Jesus Christ. Amen.

28. In fact, some of life's greatest goods can only arise out of the experience of great evils (e.g., our salvation arising out of our Lord's crucifixion). This will be a theme in my fourth volume.

Epilogue

1. Many Christians seem to think they need only the New Testament. But the New Testament itself maintains otherwise in passages such as Rom. 15:4–5; 2 Tim. 3:14–17; and (as we shall now see) preeminently in the book of Hebrews, especially in its eleventh chapter.

2. See also 1 Cor. 15:1–8, especially vv. 1–2: "Now I would remind you, brothers [and sisters], of the gospel I preached to you, which you received, in which you stand, and by which you are being saved, if you hold fast to the word I preached to you—unless you have believed in vain." At Rev. 2:10, our Lord told those in the church in Smyrna: "Do not fear what you are about to suffer. . . . Be faithful unto death, and I will give you the crown of life" (cf. Rev. 3:11–12). Enduring to the point of death or to the end of the age (see Matt. 24:3–14) is what Heb. 10 is warning us we each must do if we are to be saved.

3. I owe my understanding of Hebrews as a "word of exhortation" to Peter T. O'Brien's discussion of its genre in Peter T. O'Brien, *The Letter to the Hebrews*, Pillar New Testament Commentary (Grand Rapids, MI: Eerdmans, 2010). O'Brien writes, quoting others:

> Hebrews "begins like a treatise, proceeds like a sermon, and closes like an epistle." . . . Its purpose is hortatory, and this is repeatedly made clear by the paraenetic or exhortatory passages which are intended to warn the listeners "not to turn back from the Christian faith to the forms of piety they once knew." (20.)

He adds that such a word of exhortation "is best understood as a form of oral discourse or speech" (20), so I shall refer to his audience as his hearers.

4. Our suffering is intended to produce a kind of character that manifests itself in action over our lifetimes (see Rom. 5:3–5), and yet which may very well include some severe errors along the way (see, e.g., Ps. 51). William Sanday and

Arthur C. Headlam write that the phrase "by patience in well-doing" at Rom. 2:7 is referring to this summing up of a person's actions over a lifetime (William Sanday and Arthur C. Headlam, *A Critical and Exegetical Commentary on the Epistle to the Romans*, 5th ed. [Edinburgh: T&T Clark, 1902], 57). The Greek word for *patience* at Rom. 2:7 is the same as the word translated as *endurance* at Rom. 5:3, *patience* at 8:25, and *endurance* at Heb. 10:36 and 12:1.

5. The English Puritan Thomas Manton (1620–1677) captured the sense of this verse with a quotation from Theodore Beza: "Faith substantiates or gives a subsistence to our hopes, and demonstrates things not seen." Manton then adds, "As the matters of belief are yet to come, faith gives them a substance, a being, as they are hidden from the eyes of sense and carnal reason; so faith gives them an evidence, and does convince men of the worth of them. . . . In short, by faith things hoped for have a being; things not seen have an evidence" (Thomas Manton, *By Faith: Sermons on Hebrews 11* [1873; repr. Edinburgh: Banner of Truth, 2000], 1–2). This way of understanding faith in Heb. 11:1 complements what Paul says about hope in Rom. 5 and 8.

6. For instance, our author's declaration that "by faith we understand that the universe was created by the word of God, so that what is seen was not made out of things that are visible" (Heb. 11:3) implies that the act of creation is not something any human being could see (see Job 38:4–7). When he wrote, "By faith Noah, being warned by God concerning events as yet unseen, in reverent fear constructed an ark for the saving of his household" (v. 7), and "by faith Joseph, at the end of his life, made mention of the exodus of the Israelites and gave directions concerning his bones" (v. 22), he was of course speaking of future events that could not yet be seen.

7. Both the Old and the New Testaments imply that Abraham was impotent and make explicit that Sarah was not merely barren but beyond her childbearing years (see Gen. 17:17; 18:11; Rom. 4:19; Heb. 11:11). Here is William L. Lane's well-reasoned translation of Heb. 11:11–12: "By faith Abraham was enabled to become a father, even though Sarah herself was sterile and past the normal age of child-bearing, because he considered the one who had made the promise faithful; so it was that from this one man, and he already impotent, there were born descendants as numerous as the stars of heaven and as innumerable as the grains of sand on the seashore." William L. Lane, *Hebrews 9–13*, Word Biblical Commentary, vol. 47b (Dallas: Word, 1991), 343.

8. Ex. 2:11–15 recounts this incident in Moses's life:

> One day, when Moses had grown up, he went out to his people and looked on their burdens, and he saw an Egyptian beating a Hebrew, one of his people. He looked this way and that, and seeing no one, he struck down the Egyptian and hid him in the sand. When he went out the next day, behold, two Hebrews were struggling together. And he said to the man in the wrong, "Why do you strike your companion?" He answered, "Who made you a prince and a judge over us? Do you mean to kill me as you killed the

Egyptian?" Then Moses was afraid, and thought, "Surely the thing is known." When Pharaoh heard of it, he sought to kill Moses. But Moses fled from Pharaoh and stayed in the land of Midian. And he sat down by a well.

Does this contradict Hebrews, where it is said that Moses was unafraid of Pharaoh's anger? Perhaps the best explanation of the apparent contradiction is given in the *NIV Study Bible*, ed. Kenneth L. Barker (Grand Rapids, MI: Zondervan, 2011), in its note on Heb. 11:27:

> *By faith he left Egypt.* Probably referring to his flight to Midian when he was 40 years old . . . *not fearing the king's anger.* Exodus indicates that Moses was afraid (2:14) but does not expressly say of whom. . . . And it tells us that he fled from the pharaoh when the pharaoh tried to kill him (Ex 2:15) but does not expressly say that he fled out of fear. The author of Hebrews capitalizes on these features of the account to highlight the fact that, in his fleeing from the pharaoh, Moses was sustained by his trust in God that the liberation of Israel would come and that he would have some part in it. (2082; emphasis original.)

Ex. 2:14–15 may mean that Moses was afraid that his killing the Egyptian was known, and he fled to Midian when he learned that Pharaoh knew of it, but he did not flee because he was afraid of Pharaoh. He fled simply to stop Pharaoh from being able to do what he intended to do—namely, kill him. We may act to keep something from happening without being afraid of its happening.

9. My claims about the necessity of Abraham's and Moses's obedience for the fulfillment of God's redemptive plans may be a bit startling, since they drive home how crucial our choosing to be obedient is. Yet I am simply echoing Scripture, which emphasizes that our choices really matter, in passages such as Isa. 6:8; 56:4–5; 66:3–4; Luke 1:38; Phil. 2:12–13. See also the final words in each of our Lord's addresses to the seven churches in Rev. 2 and 3 (e.g., Rev. 2:7: "He who has an ear, let him hear what the Spirit says to the churches. *To the one who conquers*"— which of course requires us to choose to continue waging war against the world, the flesh, and the devil [see Eph. 2:2–3; Rom. 8:13; 1 Pet. 2:11]—"I will grant to eat of the tree of life, which is in the paradise of God"). The issue of how our genuinely free choices can be essential to the advancement of God's redemptive story will be front and center in the chapters on providence in my third volume.

10. K. T. Aitken writes that "the primary meaning of [*shama*] is hear sounds with the ear. Where words are heard, it implies an engagement with the mind and comes to mean listen (Gen 18:10)." (K. T. Aitken, "shama," *New International Dictionary of Old Testament Theology and Exegesis*, ed. Willem A. VanGemeren. 5 vols. [Grand Rapids, MI: Zondervan, 1997], 4:176.) He continues:

> In a variety of contexts, [*shama*] denotes listen to, heed by acting upon, or putting into practice what has been said. It may thus occur as a synonym of [*asah*], do ("Moses *listened* [*shama*] to his father-in-law and did [*asah*] everything he said," Exod 18:24). In the neg.

it means ignore, disregard (1 Sam 2:25; Jer 36:25). Where the listener is subject to the authority of the speaker, it readily comes to mean *obey* (the Rechabites "obey [*shama*] their forefather's command," Jer 35:14). . . . The Heb. constructions with [*shama*] . . . do not clearly distinguish between listening and doing. It is, therefore, often difficult to decide whether it primarily denotes a willing and attentive listening that manifests itself in obedience or whether it denotes actual obedience. (178.)

Its New Testament equivalent is: "If anyone loves me, he will keep my word, and my Father will love him, and we will come to him and make our home with him. Whoever does not love me does not keep my words. And the word that you hear is not mine but the Father's who sent me" (John 14:23–24; cf. Rom. 10:16; Gal. 5:7; 2 Thess. 3:12).

11. Of course, since their faith, hope, and obedience were the means by which God was accomplishing our redemption in Christ, they also are redeemed in Christ because they were embarked on the same trajectory as we are.

12. This isn't to say that God could not have worked in a different way to fulfill his promises but that he did not. He linked the fulfillment of his promises to real human choices to be faithful, hopeful, and thus to exercise obedience. As we shall see much more fully in examining the Scriptures on providence in my third volume, *this does not make God's redemptive plans unsure*: as the Lord declared in Gen. 18:18–19, "Abraham *shall surely* become a great and mighty nation, and all the nations of the earth shall be blessed in him. . . . *For I have chosen him*, that he may command his children and his household after him to keep the way of the Lord by doing righteousness and justice, so that the Lord may bring to Abraham what he has promised him." As I say a bit later (see p. 93), God's plans for his people have always been settled and in place *and they cannot be stymied*, as God's declaration that Abraham *shall surely* become a great and mighty nation indicates here. God *chose* Abraham to make the choice to command his children and his household after him to keep the way of the Lord. Historically, God's choice came first and then was fulfilled by Abraham's choice.

Again, Abraham chose to obey God's command to sacrifice Isaac. After he had stopped Abraham from obeying his command to take his son Isaac and offer him as a burnt offering (Gen. 22:2), God declared:

> Because you have done this and have not withheld your son, your only son, I will surely bless you, and I will surely multiply your offspring as the stars of heaven and as the sand that is on the seashore. And your offspring shall possess the gate of his enemies, and in your offspring shall all the nations of the earth be blessed, *because you have obeyed my voice.* (vv. 16–18.)

Yet we as God's saints will ultimately confess that even our obedience was enabled—but *not* forced or compelled—by God: "O Lord, you will ordain peace for us, *for you have indeed done for us all our works*" (Isa. 26:12). For although we are commanded to work out our own salvation with fear and trembling as if everything depends on what we ourselves do, we are at the same time assured that it is ultimately God who is at work within us, both to will and then to do his good purposes (see Phil. 2:12–13). We cannot completely understand how this can be. Yet our remaining faithful, hopeful, and obedient is crucial to the fulfillment of God's redemptive plans, even though the fulfillment of those plans is not ultimately at the mercy of our choices, as I shall show in volume 3.

13. Golgotha, the place where Jesus was crucified, was outside Jerusalem's gate (see John 19:17, 20). In the Old Testament, executions had to take place outside the camp or city (see Num. 15:35–36), signifying that the offender was cursed (see Lev. 24:14, 23), and thus Jesus's death by crucifixion outside Jerusalem's gate was a sign that he became cursed for us (see Gal. 3:13).

14. Geerhardus Vos put the point regarding Moses well:

> [The] phrase, *the reproach of Christ,* is explained by its usage in 13:13, "Let us therefore go forth unto him without the camp, bearing his reproach." This reproach is thus seen to be a reproach which Christ Himself first bore and which we now bear together with Him. So we must similarly interpret the reproach of Christ borne by Moses. This does not imply that Moses had a prophetic knowledge of the sufferings of the future Messiah, but rather that the reproach which Moses bore was objectively identical with the reproach suffered by Christ and His people throughout the ages. This implies, therefore, that back of all the reproaches and sufferings which God's people have endured, stood Christ. How this appeared to Moses' own subjective consciousness is told us in 11:25, "choosing rather to share ill treatment with the people of God . . ." (Geerhardus Vos, *The Teaching of the Epistle to the Hebrews* [Grand Rapids, MI: Eerdmans, 1956], 67–68.)

I owe this, as well as my understanding of the proper interpretation of Heb. 12:1, to S. M. Baugh's article "The Cloud of Witnesses in Hebrews 11," *Westminster Theological Journal,* vol. 68 (2006): 113–32.

15. I am borrowing the title of Michael W. Goheen and Craig Bartholomew's *The True Story of the Whole World: Finding Your Place in the Biblical Drama* (Grand Rapids, MI: Faith Alive Christian Resources, 2009).

16. The priority of hearing even over seeing is clear in Ps. 38. That psalm, Hans Walter Wolff tells us, is the lament of a man who sees his end approaching. To all the other symptoms of his illness is added the failure of his eyesight (v. 10). But at the height of his lamentation the psalm runs (vv. 13–14):

> But I am like a deaf man, I do not hear,
>   like a dumb man who does not open his mouth.
>
> Yea, I am like a man who no longer hears,
>   and in whose mouth there are no more answers.

The man who is threatened with becoming deaf and dumb [Wolff continues] must fear for his very humanity. *It is the hearing, the hearing above all* (vv. 13a, 14a), *that makes [us human]*—that, and the corresponding opening of the mouth, the being able to answer (vv. 13b, 14b). (Hans Walter Wolff, *Anthropology of the Old Testament* [Philadelphia: Fortress, 1974], 74; emphasis added. The remaining quotations from Wolff in this note are from p. 75.) Deuteronomy's key command is "Hear, O Israel" (6:4), which implies, Wolff writes, that "the word . . . is the essential ground of human life and its renewal." For, Wolff writes, "the ear and the mouth provide not only the specifically human exchange between [human beings]"—think here about the fact that animals don't talk—"but also that between [the Lord] and Israel, between [humankind] and its God." As Wolff concludes, "the supreme importance of the ear and of speech for true human understanding is unmistakable." This shouldn't surprise us, for the future realities on which all godly hope rests cannot be seen and so they must be foretold if they are to be known. As Wolff writes later, "the special nearness of God to man . . . comes to expression pre-eminently in the bond existing through the word" (161; see, e.g., Gen. 1:28; 9:1–7; 26:24). Much more on this in volume 3.

17. Lane, *Hebrews 9–13*, 319. He continues, "The heroic refusal of the martyrs to deny their confession bears witness to the better resurrection (11:35)." He writes of their *yearning* for what they had not yet received (emphasis original).

18. Lane translates Heb. 11:13–16:

    In accordance with the principle of faith all these persons died, not having received the fulfillment of the promises, but only seeing them and saluting them from a distance, and confessing that they were strangers and sojourners in the land. *Now people who say such things show plainly that they are expecting intensely a homeland of their own.* If they had meant that country from which they had set out, they would have had opportunity to return. But as it is they were longing for a better homeland, in other words, a heavenly one, for which reason God is not ashamed to be called their God, for he has made ready a city for them. (Lane, *Hebrews 9–13*, 343; emphasis added.)

    In other words, faith, by its very nature as trust in God's eschatological promises, acknowledges that it will never find its true fulfillment in this world.

19. F. F. Bruce observes that Hebrews' author "does not only accumulate a series of examples [in Hebrews 11]; he sets them in historical sequence so as to provide an outline of the redemptive purpose of God, advancing through the age of promise until at last in Jesus, faith's 'pioneer and perfecter,' the age of fulfillment has begun." F. F. Bruce, *The Epistle to the Hebrews* (Grand Rapids, MI: Eerdmans, 1964), 280.

20. Douglas J. Moo, *The Epistle to the Romans* (Grand Rapids, MI: Eerdmans, 1966), 509.

21. Lane, *Hebrews 9–13*, 350.

22. John Stott, *Romans: God's Good News for the World* (Downers Grove, IL: InterVarsity Press, 1994), 239. The next quotation is from the same page.

23. For lifelong singleness, see chap. 2, n. 7 and n. 16. For homosexual temptation, see Rachel Gilson, *Born Again This Way: Coming Out, Coming to Faith, and What Comes Next* (Charlotte, NC: The Good Book Co., 2020).

24. Except for those cases that involve demonic influence, Scripture limits its references to mental illness largely to depression (see, e.g., Pss. 42; 43). That Christians can become depressed is well-attested by works such as Thomas Goodwin's *A Child of Light Walking in Darkness* (c. 1647), William Bridges's *A Lifting Up for the Downcast* (1648), and Richard Winter's *The Roots of Sorrow: Reflections on Depression and Hope* (Wheaton, IL: Crossway, 1986). More recently, other kinds of mental illness have begun to be explored by Christians, such as Kathryn Greene-McCreight's exploration of her bipolar illness in *Darkness Is My Only Friend: A Christian Response to Mental Illness* (Grand Rapids, MI: Brazos, 2015). William Cowper (1731–1800), who wrote the hymn "God Moves in a Mysterious Way" and many others, was suicidally depressed several times in his life. A good, short account of his life and struggles can be found in the chapter, "'The Clouds Ye So Much Dread Are Big with Mercy': Insanity and Spiritual Songs in the Life of William Cowper," in John Piper, *The Hidden Smile of God: The Fruit of Affliction in the Lives of John Bunyan, William Cowper, and David Brainerd* (Wheaton, IL: Crossway, 2001). The entire book repays a careful read.

25. Stott observes that some Christians "talk as if . . . the body should no longer be subject to weakness, disease, pain, and decay. Yet such impatience is a form of presumption. It is to rebel against the God of history . . . who refuses to be hustled into changing his planned timetable just because we do not enjoy having to go on waiting and groaning" (Stott, *Romans*, 244).

26. C. E. B. Cranfield comments that the Greek word *logizomai*, translated as "I consider that" at the beginning of the sentence found at Rom. 8:18, "denotes a firm conviction reached by rational thought on the basis of the gospel" (C. E. B. Cranfield, *A Critical and Exegetical Commentary on the Epistle to the Romans* [Edinburgh: T. & T. Clark, 1975], 408). Later, with reference to the same Greek word at Rom. 6:11 ("So you also must consider yourselves dead to sin and alive to God in Christ Jesus"), he writes:

> [*Logizesthe*] . . . is . . . an imperative. . . . The verb . . . , as used here, denotes not a pretending ("as if"), nor a mere ideal, but *a deliberate and sober judgment on the basis of the gospel, a reasoning which is subject to the discipline of the gospel in that it accepts as its norm what God has done in Christ, the gospel-events which are only recognizable as such by faith.* (315; emphasis added.)

In *A Grief Observed* (1961; repr. New York: HarperCollins, 1994), C. S. Lewis laid bare his struggle to continue believing in spite of his wife's death. As he made clear, it was not a struggle to maintain his faith against reason but to continue to believe what he had good reason to believe in spite of his feelings. Here is one passage that exhibits the actual struggle:

> Feelings, and feelings, and feelings. Let me try thinking instead. From the rational point of view, what new factor has [Joy's] death

introduced into the problem of the universe? What grounds has it given me for doubting all that I believe? I knew already that these things, and worse, happened daily. I would have said that I had taken them into account. I had been warned—I had warned myself—not to reckon on worldly happiness. We were even promised sufferings. They were part of the programme. We were even told, "Blessed are they that mourn," and I accepted it. I've got nothing that I hadn't bargained for. Of course it is different when the thing happens to oneself, not to others, and in reality, not in imagination. Yes; but should it, for a sane man, make quite such a difference as this? No. And it wouldn't for a man whose faith had been real faith and whose concern for other people's sorrows had been real concern. (36.)

Lewis gave his reasons for believing that Christianity is true in the first chapter of his *The Problem of Pain* (1940; repr. San Francisco: Harper, 2001]), where he concluded his chapter by stating, "In a sense, [Christianity] creates, rather than solves, the problem of pain, for pain would be no problem unless, side by side with our daily experience of this painful world, we had received what we think a good assurance that ultimate reality is righteous and loving" (14). Authentic Christian belief does not fly in the face of reason. Rather, it engages in reasoning to quench unreasonable doubts.

27. C. E. B. Cranfield writes: "The whole magnificent theatre of the universe, together with all its splendid properties and all the varied chorus of sub-human life, created for God's glory, is cheated of its true fulfilment so long as man, the chief actor in the great drama of God's praise, fails to contribute his rational part. The Jungfrau and the Matterhorn and the planet Venus and all living things too, man alone excepted, do indeed glorify God in their own ways; but, since their praise is destined to be not a collection of independent offerings but part of a magnificent whole, the united praise of the whole creation, they are prevented from being fully that which they were created to be, so long as man's part is missing. . . . It is man, not the sub-human creation which is to blame for the frustration of the latter" (C. E. B. Cranfield, "Some Observations on Romans 8:19–21d," in *Reconciliation and Hope*, ed. Robert Banks [Grand Rapids, MI: Eerdmans, 1974], 227). Much more on our role in God's creation in the first two chapters of my second volume and in the last chapter of my fourth volume.

28. In Rom. 8:19 Paul personifies nature and then proffers this picture by employing the Greek term *apokaradokia*, translated as "eager longing":

The Greek term [*apokaradokia*] . . . is one of those admirable words which the Greek language easily forms. It is composed of three elements: [*kara*], *the head;* [*dokeō, dokaō, dokeuō*], *to wait for, espy* [that is, to see from afar]; and [*apo*], *from, from afar;* so: "to wait with the head raised, and the eye fixed on that a point of the horizon from which the expected object is to come." (F. Godet,

> *Commentary on the Epistle to the Romans* [Grand Rapids, MI:
> Zondervan, 1956], 313 [on Rom. 8:19].)

As John Murray comments on Rom. 5:3–4, "We glory in tribulations because they have an eschatological orientation—they serve the interests of hope. We are reminded of 1 Cor. 15:19 and advised that the complexion imparted to the perplexities of this life as in themselves the opposite of the glory to be revealed is a complexion determined by the eschatological destination of the people of God." John Murray, *The Epistle to the Romans* (Grand Rapids, MI: Eerdmans, 1968), 164.

SCRIPTURE INDEX